The *Journey of a Disciple* is not a story of the journey of any one disciple you have ever read about in the Bible. It is a story of your journey—and mine—the journey of everyone who has ever been called by our Lord Jesus Christ to be one of His disciples.

The journey of a disciple is not an easy one, but as we take the steps of that journey together, looking at the examples of those who have traveled before us, we will see how the Father calls and woos us to follow His Son; we will see how the love and sacrifice of Jesus has paved the way for us; and we will see how the Holy Spirit comes to dwell within us, empowering and equipping us for all that lies ahead, so that at the end of our journey, we will arrive at our destination in triumph.

THE JOURNEY OF A DISCIPLE

THE CHRISTIAN'S PILGRIMAGE FROM DECISION TO DISCIPLESHIP

Stuart & Jill Briscoe

Regal Books

A Division of GL Publications
Ventura, California, U.S.A.

Published by Regal Books
A Division of GL Publications
Ventura, California 93006
Printed in U.S.A.

Library of Congress Cataloging-in-Publication Data

Briscoe, D. Stuart.
    Journey of a disciple.

    1. Christian life—1960—   . I. Briscoe, Jill.
II. Title.
BV4501.2.B736   1987   248.4   87-32205
ISBN 0-8307-1210-0

2 3 4 5 6 7 8 9 10 / 94 93 92 91

Cover photo © Gilbert Beers

Rights for publishing this book in other languages are contracted by Gospel Literature International (GLINT) foundation. GLINT also provides technical help for the adaptation, translation, and publishing of Bible study resources and books in scores of languages worldwide. For further information, contact GLINT, Post Office Box 488, Rosemead, California, 91770, U.S.A., or the publisher.

CONTENTS

ACKNOWLEDGMENTS 9

INTRODUCTION 11

SECTION ONE
CALL OF A DISCIPLE

1. CORINTH: A CALL TO LOVE 17
It is the goodness of God that leads us to repentance, but it is the kindness of God that leads us to Christ.

2. EPHESUS: A GIFT OF GRACE 29
Christ had chosen him (Paul) and called him and set His grace upon him, and that was enough.

3. PATMOS: A CALLED OUT PEOPLE 41
It is a great privilege to be one of the called out people, but it is also a very great responsibility.

SECTION TWO
COMMITMENT OF A DISCIPLE

4. PHILIPPI: ATTITUDES OF A DISCIPLE 57
An attitude of prayer is essential, not only in conversion, but in opening your heart and caring for others.

5. ATHENS: STAYING TRUE TO THE CALL 69
*Everything he (Paul) told them about God
was in direct contrast to all they believed.*

6. CRETE: WEATHERING THE STORM 81
*Wherever he went . . . Paul held on to the
thought that . . . Christ keeps what is
committed to him.*

SECTION THREE

COST OF BEING A DISCIPLE

7. JERUSALEM: 95
REPENTANCE, SUBMISSION AND SURRENDER
*A vision of the risen Christ showed him (Saul) . . .
a total reversal of all that he had believed.
And that's the essence of repentance.*

8. SHILOH: YIELDING AND PRODUCING 105
*Yes is the language of relinquishment, the language
of a yielded heart.*

9. MOUNT OF OLIVES: 119
OBEDIENCE TO THE GREAT COMMISSION
*If there is going to be a valid witness, there is also
going to be some cost involved.*

SECTION FOUR

CHARACTERISTICS OF A DISCIPLE

10. MOUNT OF THE BEATITUDES: 133
LEARNING ABOUT BLESSEDNESS
*A disciple who has learned . . . blessed living
is indeed ready to go out and teach the masses.*

11. MOUNT OF THE BEATITUDES: 141
LEARNING ABOUT THE KINGDOM
The old self . . . is going to get off the throne . . .
that . . . we (might) establish the Kingdom
of God in our hearts.

12. JERUSALEM: APPROPRIATING HIS POWER 151
The Holy Spirit . . . gives us the dynamic to meet
the demands of God upon us.

EPILOGUE 165

NOTES 167

Special thanks to Kathi Mills who worked for long hours editing a video sound track into a readable manuscript.

No small feat!

INTRODUCTION

The Journey of a Disciple is not a story of any one disciple you have ever read about in the Bible. Although we will be talking quite a bit about the apostle Paul and others—John, Stephen, Hannah—the journey we are really discussing is your journey, and mine, as well as the journey of every disciple of Christ, every believer who has ever lived, who lives now, or who will live in the future. For that reason, we will not follow the lives or journeys of any of these disciples in any particular chronological order. We will, instead, concentrate on the order of the steps necessary to all of us to become faithful and effective disciples of our Lord Jesus Christ.

There has been a lot of talk about discipleship in the Church today, but just what does discipleship mean? What is a disciple? How does one become a disciple? What level of commitment is expected from a disciple? What costs are involved in discipleship? What are the recognizable characteristics of a disciple of Jesus Christ?

Section 1 of *Journey of a Disciple* deals with the call of a disciple. Our first stop on this journey will be with the apostle Paul in Corinth, where we will learn about the call of love—real love, *agape* love—on our lives. After Corinth, we will spend time with Paul in Ephesus, learning about the power and action of God's grace in our lives. When we leave Ephesus, it will be to visit the apostle John on the island of Patmos, where we will talk about being a called out people.

Section 2 is all about the commitment of a disciple. In Philippi, once again with the apostle Paul, we will be studying the attitudes that are expected of a disciple. Then, as we visit that wonderful city of Athens, we will discuss the importance of always being ready to preach the Resurrection, whatever the results or repercussions. On the lovely island of Crete, where Paul left the little harbor of Fair Havens to sail into stormy seas, we will talk about Paul's faith in the face of danger and hardship and impending shipwreck.

Section 3 brings us to the costs of discipleship. In chapter 7, we will see Paul as he was before his conversion, when he was still known as Saul of Tarsus, standing over the body of Stephen as he was martyred, and then leaving Jerusalem on the Damascus Road, where he came face-to-face with the risen Christ. At that point, we go back in time to the ancient site of Shiloh, where Hannah, a woman of prayer, begged God for a son; then, honoring her promise to God, gave up that very son for whom she had prayed so long and so faithfully. Chapter 9 takes us to the Mount of Olives, commonly believed to be the site of the Ascension. It is there we will learn about the importance of obedience to the Great Commission left us by Christ.

Section 4 covers the characteristics of a disciple. In both chapters 10 and 11, we will sit on the beautiful Mount of the Beatitudes, overlooking the Sea of Galilee, and listen, along with the disciples, as Jesus teaches in chapter 10 about a true life of blessedness; and, in chapter 11, about Kingdom living. And, finally, in chapter 12, we will return to the Old City of Jerusalem, visit the Garden Tomb, and see how the resurrection of Jesus Christ substantiates the many remarkable claims that Jesus made concerning Himself before His crucifixion. This chapter will also emphasize the fact that the very power that raised Jesus from the dead is also available to us as believers, as Christians, as disciples on a journey with our Lord Jesus Christ.

Jill will be your guide in chapter 1 as we stop in Corinth. Then I will take you on to our other stops, with the exception of our visit with Hannah at Shiloh in chapter 8. Jill has a real soft spot for this Old Testament lady, so she will relate Hannah's story to you as only another woman can. Join us now, won't you, as we embark on what I hope will be the most exciting and fulfilling journey you will ever experience.

SECTION ONE

CALL OF A DISCIPLE

CHAPTER 1

CORINTH

A CALL TO LOVE

The first place we are going to visit as we study the *call of a disciple* is Corinth. It was to the Christians in this great city that Paul wrote not one, but two letters, the summary of which is found in his *call to love,* 1 Corinthians 13.

If we could have traveled with Paul to the ancient city of Corinth some 1,900 years ago, we would be amazed to see what a magnificent and exciting city it once was. Today, looking out over the ruins of Corinth, at the piles and piles of old stones, it is hard to visualize its former beauty and grandeur. Corinth was a city that was well

Ruins at Corinth. The Acrocorinth can be seen through the pillars of an old temple. (Photo © Joyce Thimsen)

The gospel . . . was not . . . particularly attractive to a lot of people because it . . . challenge(d) them at the very roots of their life-styles.

known in the ancient world for its many splendors, including the temple of Apollo, the acropolis with its incredible temple on top of it, and the agora or marketplace, a site where crowds milled about daily.

Unfortunately, Corinth was also well known for its morality—or more accurately, its lack of it. This lack of morality was connected with the temple worship—the temple of Apollo and the temple sitting up on top of the acropolis. It is estimated that there were over 1,000 young women priestess prostitutes in the temple on the acropolis alone, and, of course, the whole of the religious observances of Corinth was tied in with all kinds of sexual immorality.

It was to this great bustling, sinful, noisy, exciting city that the apostle Paul came, and he came with some degree of trepidation. In his letters to the Corinthians, he told them quite frankly that he was fearful; he was trembling when he came to speak to the Corinthians. He knew the reputation of this city. He knew the gospel that he had to proclaim was not going to be particularly attractive to a lot of the people because it would challenge them at the very roots of their life-styles.

The church that Paul planted in Corinth was intended to play a major role in his strategy of world evangelization. Unfortunately, it hardly fulfilled his expectations.

CITY OF LOVE

Again, it was to the Christians in Corinth that Paul wrote the thirteenth chapter of 1 Corinthians, that famous portion of Scripture often referred to as the *love chapter.* Remember that Corinth was famous for being the city of love; however, it was a different kind of love than the love Paul wrote about in 1 Corinthians 13.

There are three Greek words that are used to describe love. The first is *agape,* which is God's love, the love that thinks of the other person and wants what is best for that person. It is the kind of love that says, I am concerned with your well being.

The second word for love is *phileo.* Phileo is human love, the type of love a parent has for a child, a friend has for a friend, a husband has for a wife. It is the word from which the city of Philadelphia (the city of brotherly love) gets its name.

And then there is *eros* love, that sexual, sensual sort of love for which the city of Corinth was famous. Eros love is a valid part of love, but without the phileo and agape parts of love to keep eros love under control, it is incomplete.

Eros was worshiped in Corinth. In fact, they had a temple up on top of the acropolis that exalted eros love. These worshipers of eros lived by the motto, "If it feels good, do it." Unfortunately, this attitude is becoming more and more prevalent in our society today. If it feels good, we do it. If it doesn't, we don't. If we don't feel that we love our husband or wife anymore, and maybe we love someone else instead, then we just go ahead and get a divorce and remarry. We follow our feelings.

It was to the Christians living in the midst of this city of eros worshipers that Paul wrote. He told them that, once they had become Christians, they had to begin living according to a different sort of love, agape love, the love that is primarily concerned with the other's well-being. This came as quite a shock to those Corinthian Christians.

QUALITIES OF LOVE

When Paul penned the words to 1 Corinthians 13, he was actually painting a portrait; Jesus Christ sat for that por-

*It is the goodness of God
that leads us to repentance;
it is the kindness of God that
leads us to Christ.*

trait. The words that Paul wrote paint a picture of true love, agape love. Paul described love in action. If love doesn't act, it's not really love. Eros love follows its feelings, satisfies its own desires. Paul told the Corinthian Christians that real love, the sort of love they needed to begin showing in their lives, was patient and kind. The King James Version of 1 Corinthians 13 says that love "suffereth long, and is kind" (see v. 4).

Love is good at suffering. Are you good at suffering? Am I? Do we suffer patiently? Love is patient; it waits out the suffering. That is God's love. God is always patient. And while He's being patient, He's also being very kind. Kindness is the active side of patience.

Love Is Action

How do we put this agape love into action in our lives? Why not begin at home with our own families? I remember when our teenagers were giving us a little bit of a runaround. Our daughter, in particular, was becoming quite a challenge. We tried everything. We read the Dobson books, watched all the films, did everything all the experts told us to do, but we just couldn't get her to respond. Our relationship was deteriorating. And then a dear friend suggested that we try a little kindness. Our first reaction was that our daughter didn't deserve any kindness, but we decided to try it anyway. Amazingly enough, it worked!

We must never forget that it is the goodness of God that leads us to repentance; it is the kindness of God that leads us to Christ. We do not have the ability to exercise that degree of kindness within ourselves, but the Holy Spirit gives us that ability when we seek His help. Our phileo love (the type of love a parent has for a child) runs out quickly in the face of a hostile, unresponsive teenager; but agape love, God's love, never runs out. Paul explained to the Corinthians that if they really wanted to love, they had to suffer long and patiently, showing kindness even toward people who were irritating and ungrateful.

Love Is Selfless

He also told them that agape love "does not envy" (v. 4). There are two parts to envy. The first part says, "I want what you've got." That's coveting. If you don't let God deal with that envy, that coveting, it works its way down into deep, bedrock jealousy, which says, "And I don't want you to have it either."

Newly married couples often fall into this trap of envy, covetousness and jealousy, particularly if they've come from a background where they had everything they wanted. Suddenly, they're married and they no longer have as much as they did when they still lived at home with Mom and Dad. Before long they find themselves thinking, "I want what Mom and Dad have," or "I want what so-and-so has," and then their marriage can get into trouble.

The only thing that can overcome envy, covetousness and jealousy is the love of God, because real love, agape love, doesn't envy, doesn't covet, and is not jealous. God gives, asking nothing in return. When the Lord Jesus Christ is in control of our lives, then we are content with what we have. Paul had learned this, and expressed it very well in Philippians 4:11-13:

> *I have learned to be content whatever the circumstances. I know what it is to be in need, and I know what it is to have plenty. I have learned the secret of being content in any and every situation, whether well fed or hungry, whether living in plenty or in want. I can do everything through him who gives me strength.*

I came from a wealthy home. When I married Stuart, an evangelist and missionary, my life-style changed drastically. But I learned to be content with the things I had, because I had Jesus. And I want to tell you that I'd rather live in my cottage with Jesus than in my castle without Him. I lived for 18 years without Christ, and it wasn't any fun. I know what it is to have everything and be empty, and I know what it is to have very little and to be full. I know what it is to be content with the things that I have, because God's love filled me and that's enough.

Love Is Humble

Paul was writing to the Corinthian Christians about these things. He told them they weren't to be proud, because love "does not boast, it is not proud" (1 Cor. 13:4). The King James Version says love "is not puffed up." The word in the Greek means windbag. Love is not a windbag. Are we windbags? Do we always talk about ourselves? Love never talks about itself. Love is quiet. Love tiptoed onto this earth, was born in a manger, didn't flaunt itself, didn't strut around the world. Jesus was humble. He did miracles. He healed lepers. But then He would say, Don't tell anyone. Shh, I don't want them to know. When we do something great, don't we want everyone to know? If we ever performed a miracle, wouldn't we want to tell everyone? Love doesn't want everyone to know what it has done; it doesn't need to make an entrance, be on a platform or be noticed, because love isn't proud.

Then Paul told the Corinthians that love does not "behave itself unseemly" (v. 5, *KJV*). Love has good manners. Love says, "After you," because love isn't pushy; it doesn't have to be first. This is God's sort of love that Paul was describing to a group of Corinthians who had known nothing before except following their own desires, their own whims.

Love Is Forgiving

Paul also told them that love "keeps no record of wrongs" (v. 5); it "does not delight in evil but rejoices with the truth" (v. 6). That's an interesting thought, isn't it? Love keeps no record of wrongs. The Greek word means it doesn't keep running records. There are some of us who have a hard time forgiving because we have so much to forgive. Some of us have suffered terrible injustices, terrible wrongs. Do we keep a running book of those wrongs? Do we think of them constantly, go to bed with them, get up with them in the morning?

Once, when Stuart visited a witch doctor's house, he noticed a lot of strange objects hanging around the roof. When he asked the witch doctor what they were, he was told they were reminders of the things people had done against him. The witch doctor had hung them there to make sure he never forgot the wrongs done him by others.

What have you got hanging around the roof of your mind? Love deals with those reminders. Love helps to forgive, because you cannot love and hate at the same time. If you are exercising God's love, agape love, you will forgive others, and with that forgiveness, your bad feelings toward them will begin to fade. You can count on it. Paul said, "Love never fails" (v. 8). If you act on God's love, it will always accomplish what He has promised.

God took a lot of people in the immoral, pagan city of Corinth, and He changed them. He changed them by putting within their hearts the ability to love as He loves—not eros love, not even phileo love, but agape love—the love that never fails.

BODY OF LOVE

Once we, as those early Christians in Corinth, have been called to love, how do we exercise that love? How do we use and demonstrate that love to others? The Church of Jesus Christ is intended to be the Body of Christ. A body is the means whereby a spiritual entity functions in a physical environment. If we are to be the Body of Christ, allowing a spiritual Christ to function in our world, doing the things that He always did, it is obvious that no one man will have all the abilities or the gifts that are necessary to do so. That's why the Body, made up of many gifted individuals, is so important. There will be one who can teach as Christ taught, one who can heal as Christ healed, another one who can evangelize as Christ evangelized (see 1 Cor. 12:4-11). It is important that, in the community of believers, we encourage each other in our ministries, as well as in the identification and utilization of our individual gifts.

Identifying Your Gifts

You may be wondering, How do I find out what my gifts are? I would suggest a very simple method. Ask God to lead you into an area of ministry. Ask God to give you an area of concern, and then move into that area of ministry, move into that area of concern; then ask God to assist you in doing what you think needs to be done. Trust Him to lead you in the right direction. Take another believer with you. Ask that believer to observe you, to criticize you, to speak the truth in love to you. And, very quickly, as you do the ministry that you feel called to, you will find out whether you are gifted for it.

It may well be that you will discover you have no gift in that particular area of ministry, after all. Don't be discouraged. God has gifted you for the ministry that He wants for you and, in time, you will find out what it is. However, if you just sit around waiting for a gift or trying to figure out what your gift is, the chances are that you won't do anything. But if you step out in faith and embark on a ministry, sooner or later you will begin to discover what your gifts are; you will be encouraged by other believers who affirm you in your ministry; you will see evidence of God's blessing upon your ministry; and you will have a deeply rooted sense of peace and well being and holy joy as you engage in that ministry.

Paul had a gift of teaching, although he probably had many other gifts also. As I said, I believe it is important for each of us to identify all our spiritual gifts. However, I believe there is something more important than simply identifying our ministry; and that is, once we have discovered what our ministry is, we can also be absolutely certain that God will gift us to carry out that ministry effectively (see Eph. 4:11-13). But the Bible teaches something very powerful here. It says that every believer is gifted by the Holy Spirit. But it also tells us that our gifts will differ, as Paul explained to the Corinthians in 1 Corinthians 12. Therefore, it is wrong for Christians to say that they are not gifted. It is equally incorrect for people to think that others ought to have the gift that they themselves have.

Do you know what your ministry is? Have you identified your gifts? Are you encouraged in the exercise of them? As you move into ministry in answer to your call to love, remember to encourage others as they also seek to minister in the name of Christ.

SOMETHING TO THINK ABOUT

1. How have you answered God's call on your life to love? How can you answer it on a continual basis, daily, even when that call deals with a person or a situation that is unpleasant or difficult?
2. As you study Paul's letters to the Corinthians, particularly 1 Corinthians 13, what qualities of agape love do you recognize in your own life? What qualities do you realize are lacking and need a work of grace to be developed in you?

CHAPTER 2

EPHESUS
A GIFT OF GRACE

Travel in the Mediterranean today is much more comfortable than it was in Paul's day, and circumstances for the modern tourist are very different than those he encountered. Nevertheless, the scenery has changed little from what Paul saw, and the life-style of the people today bears many similarities to that of his day. When Paul sailed from Corinth to Ephesus, he passed the many picturesque islands that now dot the Aegean Sea with grandeur and spectacle for the modern tourist, just as they filled the sea with danger for the ancient mariners.

WHAT IT USED TO BE

After the welcome respite of that voyage, Paul and his friends arrived in Ephesus, ready for the next phase of

their ministry. Although the city of Ephesus is now a magnificent ruin, it certainly wasn't that way when Paul first got there. At that time, there was a mile-long road that stretched from the port right to the center of the city. In the city's heyday, the road was covered with marble. On each side of the road were huge columns, which supported a roof. Under the shade of that roof were crowds of people, coming and going into the city.

The city of Ephesus was a large, hustling, bustling center of activity; but through the years, the port ceased to be usable, the city began to fade away, and the once glorious city of Ephesus fell into ruin.

The passing away of Ephesus reminds me of something the Lord said to John in the book of Revelation. He told the church in Ephesus:

> *You have forsaken your first love. Remember the height from which you have fallen! Repent and do the things you did at first. If you do not repent, I will come to you and remove your lampstand from its place* (Rev. 2:4,5).

There is no longer a church in Ephesus. There is no city of Ephesus. It is a desolate, discouraging place; and yet, there is enough left to remind us of what used to be.

A SHORT STAY

While still in Corinth, Paul had met Aquila and Priscilla. They shared the same trade, the same faith, and together they ministered in the name of Christ in Corinth. When

A portion of the mile-long road at Ephesus. (Photo © Gilbert Beers)

time came for Paul to move on, Aquila and Priscilla went with him. In all probability, when they arrived in Ephesus, they made their way into the city along that mile-long road.

Although Paul had his heart set on going to Ephesus from Corinth, he didn't want to stay in Ephesus long. He felt he needed to make his way on to Jerusalem so that he might report back to the churches from which he had come on his missionary journey. So, Paul asked Aquila and Priscilla to remain in Ephesus, presumably to establish a business, and then he left.

But, before he left Aquila and Priscilla behind, Paul, as was his usual custom, visited the synagogue in Ephesus. After the difficult times he'd had in Corinth and in other places, he must have been rather gratified to have been warmly received by the people in the synagogue. These people were intrigued by the message he brought concerning Jesus, about His death and resurrection. They didn't immediately accept what Paul had to say, but they were interested and very eager for him to stay with them for a while.

In spite of their warm welcome, however, Paul felt he must leave. He was anxious to get back to Jerusalem, to his beloved Antioch of Syria, so that he could communicate once again with the church that had commended him to the ministry. And so, bidding farewell to his dear friends Aquila and Priscilla, Paul left Ephesus after only a very brief stay.

A CALL TO RETURN

Paul made the trip back to Caesarea, spent some time in Jerusalem and in Antioch, but then the old desire to keep moving began to burn in him once again. He struck out through the regions of Galatia, where he had earlier founded churches and, I'm sure, experienced times of great joy as well as times of heavy sorrow. All of us who have been called to a ministry (and that means each and every one of us who has answered God's call to love) know what it is to be encouraged when we see the seeds we've planted blossoming and flourishing; we also know what it is to be discouraged when there seems to be no fruit at all. I'm sure this was the case with Paul as he visited the churches in Derbe and Lystra and Iconium, among others.

After these stops, Paul moved on, making a great loop and sweeping down south again until he arrived once more in Ephesus. While he had been away, Aquila and Priscilla had been able to establish their business, so Paul was able to come right in and join with them in the tent-making trade that would be their means of support while they engaged in ministry in Ephesus.

ATTENDING TO BUSINESS

Upon Paul's arrival in Ephesus the second time, he immediately "entered the synagogue and spoke boldly there for three months, arguing persuasively about the kingdom of God" (Acts 19:8). Paul didn't waste time. He didn't beat around the bush. He got right down to the business at hand. But even though he argued persuasively, verse 9 tells us, "Some of them became obstinate; they refused to believe and publicly maligned the Way. So Paul left them."

Paul knew what his business was—to proclaim the gospel. For three months, he argued persuasively with these people, trying to help them understand and accept his message. But he also knew that, although he must proclaim the gospel to them, he could not force them to

Paul was so overwhelmed, so thrilled by the sheer grace that God had shown to him, that he felt motivated by it.

believe. Therefore, when they became obstinate and refused to believe, he moved on. He left the synagogue, took his disciples with him, and went over to the lecture hall of Tyrannus to continue his ministry.

Verse 10 goes on to say, "This went on for two years, so that all the Jews and Greeks who lived in the province of Asia heard the word of the Lord." Even though Paul met opposition to his message in the synagogue, he did not let that discourage him. He just moved to another spot and continued to preach the gospel. And he didn't stop until "all the Jews and Greeks who lived in the province of Asia heard the word of the Lord." Do you have that sort of tenacity? Do I? Do we *hang tough* despite opposition and hardships until we have accomplished what God has called us to do? When things don't go as planned, do we give up, or do we make adjustments and continue on with our ministry?

TRIUMPHING IN TRIBULATION

Paul's ministry in Ephesus was not an easy one. Although God gave him great successes—"God did extraordinary miracles through Paul" (v. 11) and, as we've already noted, he was able to get the Word of God out to every Jew and Greek in the area—there were many in Ephesus who hated and feared Paul, even to the point of inciting riots and public demonstrations against him. But Paul persevered.

That doesn't mean that he was never tempted to give up. In fact, we're not really sure about all the details of what happened to Paul in Ephesus. In his Epistles he mentions some terribly trying circumstances during his stay there, including being thrown to wild beasts (see 1 Cor. 15:32). He talks about being terribly depressed, about facing overwhelming circumstances. Some believe he was imprisoned during part of his stay in Ephesus; others believe he was physically beaten; still others believe he was literally thrown to wild beasts and survived. We can't really say for certain, but there is enough evidence in his writings to indicate that he was under much pressure during this time.

Whatever the problems and pressures Paul faced during his stay in Ephesus, his commitment to the gospel, his call to love, enabled him to overcome these obstacles and to be able to say to the Ephesians:

> *Finally, be strong in the Lord and in his mighty power. Put on the full armor of God so that you can stand against the devil's schemes. For our struggle is not against flesh and blood, but against the rulers, against the authorities, against the powers of this dark world and against the spiritual forces of evil in the heavenly realms . . . . Pray also for me, that whenever I open my mouth, words may be given me so that I will fearlessly make known the mystery of the gospel, for which I am an ambassador in chains. Pray that I may declare it fearlessly, as I should* (Eph. 6:10-12, 19, 20).

The Source of His Triumphs

Looking at all the trials and tribulations that Paul suffered during his lifetime, it is natural to wonder what it was that kept motivating this man. Even while he ministered in Ephesus, watching a new church being formed, he still carried the burden of all the other churches at the same time. But Paul himself told us the source of his strength, that motivating factor, in his second letter to the Corinthi-

*C*hrist had chosen him (Paul) and called him and set His grace upon him, and that was enough.

ans, where he described his pleading with God to remove the thorn in his flesh (see 2 Cor. 12:7,8). God answered him, "My grace is sufficient for you, for my power is made perfect in weakness" (v.9). Paul then responded, "That is why, for Christ's sake, I delight in weaknesses, in insults, in hardships, in persecutions, in difficulties. For when I am weak, then I am strong" (v. 10). It was God's all-encompassing grace that buoyed Paul above his countless pains and problems.

OVERWHELMED BY GRACE

Paul was so overwhelmed, so thrilled by the sheer grace that God had shown to him, that he felt motivated by it. It called him onward, spurred him forward. Paul said that it was the grace of God that equipped him for all the things he had to face. He knew that, in himself, he could do nothing; yet Christ had chosen him and called him and set His grace upon him, and that was enough.

The fact that God had called him was a constant source of amazement to Paul. He considered himself unworthy to spread the gospel, particularly in light of his past persecution of the Church. In 1 Corinthians 15:9,10 Paul said:

> *For I am the least of the apostles and do not even deserve to be called an apostle, because I persecuted the church of God. But by the grace of God I am what I am, and his grace to me was not without effect. No, I worked harder than all of them— yet not I, but the grace of God that was with me.*

Paul realized that it was God's grace that made him an apostle, God's grace that enabled him to preach the gospel; because of that, he was able to accept himself just as he was, past track records, imperfections, human frailties and all. Have we come to that point in our Christian walk? Can we accept God's forgiveness for the past, trusting Him to work through us in spite of that past? Can we trust Him to continue to work through us in spite of our frailties and shortcomings, believing that the work He has begun in us He will also finish?

Paul believed it, and he declared it in his letter to the Philippians: "Being confident of this, that he who began a good work in you will carry it on to completion until the day of Christ Jesus" (1:6). Believe it. Accept it. Say it along with Paul. "By the grace of God I am what I am." We are not good enough or strong enough to make it on our own, but with God's grace, we can make it. Indeed, we will make it.

As Paul said in his second letter to the Corinthians, "God is able to make all grace abound to you, so that in all things at all times, having all that you need, you will abound in every good work" (2 Cor. 9:8). It was this sense of high and noble privilege, this promise by Almighty God to meet Paul's every need and to prosper him in his work, that kept Paul ministering, not only in Ephesus, but elsewhere as well.

SOMETHING TO THINK ABOUT

1. What times in your life can you remember doubting the sufficiency of God's grace to solve your problem, meet your need, carry you through a time of great trial and testing? Now, can you think of even one time when, after letting go and trusting God's grace, He failed you?
2. How does this affect the way you will handle future

problems and trials? How is it easier to trust the grace of God, knowing that He has never failed you or forsaken you in the past? In what ways will it give you more confidence as you go forward in ministry with Him?

CHAPTER 3

PATMOS

A Called Out People

As we leave the apostle Paul for a while to visit John on the island of Patmos, we are reminded that it wasn't only Paul who risked life and limb to preach the gospel. John was sentenced to exile on Patmos for his testimony of Christ, and it was there that he wrote the book of Revelation.

As we read the book of Revelation, we tend to think that it was written to us as individuals and, of course, there is much to be appropriated by us individually from that book; however, it's important for us to remember that this book was directed to the angels (leaders) of the churches. There were seven different churches at that time, which had been founded around Ephesus, and it was to these communities of believers that John wrote.

The reason I believe it is so important that we bear in mind that John was writing to these seven different churches rather than to individuals is that Christianity is not to be lived on an individual level only. Certainly, we recognize the beautiful privilege that we have as individuals who are related personally to Christ. But in addition

to that, we have both the privilege and the responsibility of being related to others who themselves are also related to Christ.

WHO IS THE CHURCH?

I remember years ago, we were standing on the Acropolis in Athens one long, hot afternoon, when we met a young, knowledgeable Greek who told us some things we have never forgotten. For instance, he told us that in ancient Greece it was a great privilege to be a member of the township or the city-state of Athens. Because it was a privilege, it was also a responsibility. Part of that responsibility was that, when the affairs of the city had to be decided, it was necessary for the citizens to leave their work and to go to a special place to discuss and to decide the particular business affairs in question.

The Called Out People

There is a lovely hillside near Mars Hill in Athens, and it was to this hillside that the people were called away to settle city-state business. The Greek word for "calling out" or "calling away" is *ekklesia.* It is the word from which we get *ecclesiastical. Ekklesia* is also the Greek word translated church in the New Testament. Therefore, every time we use the name church, we need to remember that we are talking about a called out people.

Now, in the same way that the people of ancient Athens were called out of the marketplace up onto the hillside

A view from the Isle of Patmos, one of the Sporades Islands located about 28 miles southwest of the island of Samos and about the same distance from Asia Minor Coast. (Photo © Cyrus Nelson)

as the *ekklesia* to deal with the business of the city, so believers have been called by the Lord Jesus out of the world in which they live into a new community—the *ekklesia*, the church, the called out people of God. With that calling out comes many privileges and responsibilities.

The Private People

This young man we were talking to on the Acropolis told us something else that was very fascinating. He said that sometimes, when the meetings were called, some of the people didn't want to leave their normal affairs; they just wanted to continue on with their ordinary business. And so they stayed on in the marketplace, the agora, and went on with their personal, private affairs.

These people, understandably, were not looked upon very highly because they wanted all the privileges of being a part of the city-state of Athens, but they didn't want to accept the responsibilities that went with those privileges. There was a special name for these people: they were called *private people*, because they were more interested in their personal, private, individual affairs than they were in the affairs of the corporate whole, or the body of people. The Greek word for a private person was, ironically enough, *idiotes*, from which we get our contemporary word "idiot." Now, I don't want to offend anyone, but may I suggest that our churches have too many idiots in them. Let me explain.

It is possible, as individuals, to be called into fellowship with the Lord Jesus and with other believers, to be called to be part of the church; yet, having been called into that fellowship, some of us are so interested in our own personal affairs that we don't want to tear ourselves away from them long enough to get involved in the affairs of others.

EXTENDING OUR COMMITMENT

Let me ask you something. Do you have a commitment to the Lord Jesus? I hope so. Now, let me ask you something else. Do you have a commitment to a body of believers? Do you have a commitment to an ekklesia?

Years ago, when I was younger and slightly more foolish, I used to say something like, "I'm all in favor of the Lord Jesus, but I've no time for His Church."

Then somebody challenged me on this point one day and said to me, "How can you be all in favor of the Lord Jesus, yet not be in favor of what He's all in favor of?"

Well, I wasn't too sure what he was talking about, but he pointed out something to me. He said that the Lord Jesus had made a commitment, and that commitment was to build His Church. This commitment of Christ to the Church is something that Christians need to understand. If we have a commitment to Him, we need to have a commitment to the Church that He is building.

Now, I fully recognize that some people will say, "Well, I have a commitment to the Church, that great big universal, mystical body of believers, and that's enough." It isn't enough. Because, while it is true that the Scriptures talk about the Church—that mystical, universal body—it is equally true that they talk about individual churches, local churches, in geographical locations, planted among groups of people: the church of Smyrna, the church of Pergamum, the church of Laodicea, the Church at Ephesus, and, of course, all the other of the seven churches to which the book of Revelation was addressed.

Join a Local Church

So we must recognize that, if we have a commitment to Christ and to His universal body, the Church, we need to

*T*he called out people . . .
are intended to be alternate
societies in the midst of a fragmented society.

have a commitment to a local body of believers, as well. If I were to ask you what is God's answer to a fallen individual, you'd answer immediately, Christ! If I were then to ask you what is God's answer to a fragmented society, the answer would be, the Church! In other words, the called out people especially belonging to the Lord, people living in geographical locations as special, unique communities, are intended to be alternate societies in the midst of a fragmented society. To what end? To show society what society is intended to be.

STANDING TOGETHER

On Patmos, the Lord spoke to John. He told him to write to the leaders of the seven churches. He said to remind them that they were to function as churches, that they were to function on the basis of love, that they were to be faithful to the Lord and faithful to each other, that they were to be mutually supportive, that they were to stand firm together as they confronted the tremendous pressures that were to come their way. A similar message needs to be reiterated to the contemporary Church. It is necessary that we stand together. It is necessary that we demonstrate a quality of love among ourselves that will be attractive and winsome to those who are not members of the Body of Christ, not a part of the Church, so that they can observe the way we behave and be attracted by it.

The Tragedy of Division

What a scandal it is when our churches are full of people who don't speak to each other! What a tragedy when churches split, when schisms come, when people refuse to have anything to do with each other, when they become

It is a great privilege to be one of the called out people, but it is also a very great responsibility.

uncooperative. It is contrary to all that the Church is intended to be. We need to think of the message that the Lord sent to those seven churches through John, and we need to examine our own hearts to see if we are really excited about the total commitment of ourselves, not only to the Lord Jesus and to the Church as a whole, but to a local body of believers, called out from the world to be a unique society, showing those outside the Church what society should truly be like. It is a great privilege to be one of the called out people, but it is also a very great responsibility.

The Church is not bricks and mortar, even though imposing structures are used by people around the world for worship and service. No, the Church is something we *are*, not somewhere we *go*.

FIRST LOVE

After Paul had completed his ministry in Ephesus, John, the beloved disciple, started his. Deeply revered, a man of many years experience, he was known for coming into a community of believers and saying, "Brothers, love one another." But John was eventually sent into exile from Ephesus to Patmos, a beautiful little piece of real estate, fifteen square miles of rock, situated in the center of the gorgeous Aegean Sea. While John was on that island in exile, he had his remarkable vision, and that vision was recorded under the inspiration of the Holy Spirit. Now, of course, it is known as the book of Revelation.

The Good News, the Bad News

Part of that vision that John received from the Lord was a letter to the Christians in Ephesus. He started the letter in this way:

> *I know your deeds, your hard work and your per-*
> *severance. I know that you cannot tolerate*
> *wicked men, that you have tested those who claim*
> *to be apostles but are not, and have found them*
> *false. You have persevered and have endured*
> *hardships for my name, and have not grown*
> *weary* (Rev. 2:2,3).

What he was actually saying was, first the good news. The good news about the people in Ephesus was that they worked hard for the Lord, they labored. They had a good attitude, they were patient, they stuck out their Christianity with a steady tenacity. They also were intolerant of evil; they were not fooled by carnal Christians, those who professed Christianity but lived licentiously. They were commended for all that by the Lord Jesus in the beginning of His letter to them, but then He gets down to business.

"Nevertheless," He says to them at the beginning of verse 4 (*KJV*)—anytime you see a *nevertheless* in the Bible, be ready for something big—"Nevertheless I have somewhat against thee." Now, the bad news. What was the bad news? "Thou hast left thy first love" (v. 4, *KJV*). The *New International Version* says, "You have forsaken your first love." Have you ever thought about that? Have you ever realized that Jesus Christ is concerned, that He has something against us if we forsake our first love?

First Love Shines

What is first love? First love is wanting to gaze into someone's eyes; first love is taking risks; first love is wanting to be with that special someone every possible moment; first love makes allowances. My wife, Jill, has written a poem about first love, about how she felt when she first came to the Lord Jesus and how her heart was full of first love for Him.

No More Grey

by Jill Briscoe

No more grey, Lord;
colors crowd my life,
soft colors of love.
No more sterile air;
fresh winds blow
through my mind.
See my thoughts now,
falling into line like
rows of orderly soldiers,
marching merrily to war,
sure of victory,
fighting for a cause.
No more empty spaces to live in;
Jesus is here.
Sweet friend,
determined to
make me His confidant.
No more grey, Lord;
colors crowd my life,
soft colors of love. [1]

That's first love. Is that what's in your heart for the Lord Jesus? Or have you, too, forsaken your first love? Maybe you lost it somewhere along the way and didn't even realize it. How do you keep it? How do you get it back? You can't work it up through your own determination. It's the Holy Spirit who sheds abroad His love in our hearts that keeps that first love burning. If we've lost our first love, we must repent. That's the message that Jesus told John to write to the church in Ephesus. "Repent and do the things you did at first" (Rev. 2:5). Repent. Do the things you did at first before you lost your first love.

What were those things? The sort of things you do when you first love someone. Being a Christian and loving Jesus means you don't care who knows. You talk about Him all the time because you love Him so much. If we don't repent and do those things that we did at first, Jesus says, "I will come to you and remove your lampstand from its place" (v. 5). What does that mean? That we will no longer shine, because first love shines.

The Cry of a Loving Heart

Incidentally, first love for Jesus means first love for everyone else. Have you ever thought about having a first-love relationship with other believers? If you have a first-love relationship with God through Christ, then it will spill over and you'll have first-love relationships with other people—love that makes allowances, love that thinks of the other first. First love.

This was a real heart cry from the Lord Jesus, not only to the church at Ephesus, but to the other six churches, as well—a cry of concern for the suffering and persecution that He knew would soon come to them. Without their first love burning in their hearts, He knew they would have a hard time remaining faithful.

There are so many things that can divert and distract believers. There are so many things that will lead us into areas where we don't belong. It is so easy for us to grow cold. It is so easy for us to become absorbed with things of secondary importance, so easy to forget the commitments we have made.

We, in the western world, have been spared many of

the most difficult trials that some in other parts of the world face on a daily basis. And yet, by the same token, we have so many things crowded into our busy and comfortable lives that, very often, the Lord Jesus is pushed into a corner of our existence.

In speaking to the church at Laodicea, Jesus says, "Here I am! I stand at the door and knock. If anyone hears my voice and opens the door, I will come in and eat with him, and he with me" (Rev. 3:20). This verse is often used to lead someone to Christ, which is fine. But, if read in its proper context, the Lord Jesus is really talking to a church, and, in essence, He's saying, You seem to be managing very well without me. I'd love to get back in, to be an integral part of your fellowship. It is my body, and if only someone would open the door and let me in, what a transformation you would see!

This is the thrust of the message that came from Patmos. There is a coming day to which we can look forward, there is an opportunity coming when we'll be able to see God and share with Him in His eternal kingdom. Surely, out of a loving heart, the cry of the Apostle as he concludes the book of Revelation should be on our lips at all times: "Even so, come, Lord Jesus!"

SOMETHING TO THINK ABOUT

1. How can you know that you have been called out by God to be a part of His Church, to live a life that will reflect God's love and grace to an unbelieving world? How can you prevent the cares of this world from tying you down so that you cannot—or will not—answer when our Lord calls?

2. How can you be sure that your first love for the Lord Jesus Christ still burns strong in your heart? How can you be sure you haven't lost that first love? Why is it important that you cry out with the Apostle John, "Even so, come, Lord Jesus"?

SECTION TWO

COMMITMENT
OF A DISCIPLE

CHAPTER 4

PHILIPPI

ATTITUDES OF A DISCIPLE

The ancient city of Philippi was named after a great king, Philip of Macedonia, the father of Alexander the Great, who ruled the city for some time; but eventually Philippi fell into the hands of the Romans. One of the victors of the battle that secured Philippi for Rome was Mark Antony, who subsequently came and lived in the area, turning the city into a Roman colony.

When Paul arrived in Philippi, he undoubtedly walked up the Via Ignatia (the remains of which still exist), straight into the massive Roman forum. He was surrounded on every side by splendid buildings and elaborate temples. Latin was the language he heard all around him. He could not have set foot in the city without immediately sensing the Roman nature of Philippi.

Ruins of the massive Roman Forum in Philippi.
(Photo © Gilbert Beers)

AN ATTITUDE OF PRAYER

The first thing Paul did upon arriving in Philippi was to inquire whether or not there was a synagogue. When he learned there was no synagogue (a synagogue could not be established without a minimum of ten male Jews), he searched for a place where the local God-fearing Jews would meet. Acts 16:13-15 tells us:

> *On the Sabbath we went outside the city gate to the river, where we expected to find a place of prayer. We sat down and began to speak to the women who had gathered there. One of those listening was a woman named Lydia, a dealer in purple cloth from the city of Thyatira, who was a worshiper of God. The Lord opened her heart to respond to Paul's message. When she and the members of her household were baptized, she invited us to her home.*

I've always found it fascinating that Paul had a vision of a man of Macedonia calling him over to help (see Acts 16:9,10), but when he arrived, he started his ministry there among women. It seems incredible that, with only ten male Jews required to establish a synagogue, Paul was unable to find one in the entire city of Philippi. But you'll notice the Scripture says that, when they went down to the river looking for a place of prayer, they found women gathered there. Where were the men?

Prayer Precedes Conversion

One of the women present that day, Lydia, listened to what Paul had to say and, when the Lord opened her heart, she responded to the message of the gospel. And then, when she and the members of her family were baptized, she invited Paul and his companions to her home. One of the things that struck me about Lydia's acceptance of Paul's gospel message was the fact that she had been at a place of prayer before Paul came and spoke to her and the other women. Prayer always precedes conversion.

Sometimes, when someone comes to faith in Christ seemingly from nowhere, I stop and wonder for a moment how it could have happened. And then I think of my wife. Jill came from a background where people had not been raised in the teachings of the Church; and yet, one day, she discovered she had a praying grandfather. When someone accepts the gospel message and turns to Christ, almost always you will find someone, somewhere, standing in the shadows praying, whether it be a relative, a neighbor or a friend.

Things really haven't changed much since Paul's day, have they? When Paul went down to the river to the place where people gathered to pray, he found a group of women. Doesn't it seem that it's usually the women who are the most faithful about praying? Again, where were the men? Hadn't Paul come to Macedonia looking for the man he had seen in his vision? But when he found only women at the river, he didn't get discouraged. He didn't ignore them and go looking for the men. He simply preached his message, trusting God for the outcome.

Eventually, Paul did find the men of the city, because, at the end of chapter 16, after Paul and Silas had been let out of prison, verse 40 tells us, "They went to Lydia's house, where they met with the brothers and encouraged them." It's a great way to evangelize—start with the women and, eventually, you'll reach the men, as well.

Paul wasn't discouraged when he found only a small group of women at the place of prayer. God uses each and

An attitude of prayer is essential, not only in conversion, but in opening your heart and caring for others.

every one of us. Never think of yourself as insufficient to accomplish something; don't think of yourself as *only one*—think of yourself as the *first one*. Lydia was the first one—the first one whose heart God had prepared. From that first prepared heart, the church of Philippi was born.

Prayer Prepares for Ministry

Not only does prayer precede conversion, it also prepares the heart for ministry. God had been preparing Lydia's heart through her times in prayer, and when she heard Paul's message, she accepted it and was converted. Immediately afterward, she urged them to come to her home. You know, when you're a praying person, you're a hospitable person. Your attitude is one of concern for others. Your home becomes a place of refuge, as Lydia's home became for Paul and his companions.

What does it mean to have an open home? First of all, it means hard work. In those days there were no washing machines or any other time-saving appliances. When you invited someone into your home, you took their clothes down to the river and washed them by hand. Having an open home isn't easy. It costs something. Are you willing to open your home and offer it to others so that they can stop and rest and be encouraged and maybe even find Christ for the first time while they're there?

An attitude of prayer is essential, not only in conversion, but in opening your heart and caring for others, as Lydia did. And what a mighty work God was able to accomplish there in Philippi through the apostle Paul because Lydia had been spending time in prayer.

AN ATTITUDE OF CONFIDENCE

Things continued to go well in Philippi after Paul's meeting with Lydia, and a small fellowship of believers was born. But Satan can't stand it when things are going well for Christians, and he always attacks at that point. Sometimes, however, when he attacks, he overreaches himself and things backfire. That's exactly what happened in this case.

There was a young woman in Philippi who was demon-possessed; she was involved in the occult arts and her divination powers were being used as a source of income by a group of unscrupulous men. When the evil spirit within the young woman began to harass Paul, taunting him and crying out to all who would listen, "These men are servants of the Most High God, who are telling you the way to be saved" (Acts 16:17), he tried to ignore her. Perhaps he felt he wasn't ready yet for that type of confrontation. However, one day he could stand the continual harassment no longer. Paul turned to her and said to the spirit within her, "In the name of Jesus Christ I command you to come out of her!" (v. 18). The verse goes on to say, "At that moment the spirit left her."

When the girl's owners realized that they had lost their source of income, they were furious. They dragged Paul into the marketplace among a great crowd of people to face the authorities, saying, "These men are Jews, and are throwing our city into an uproar by advocating customs unlawful for us Romans to accept or practice" (vv. 20,21).

Now, Roman law forbade the flogging of Roman citizens, and Paul was a Roman citizen. But either he didn't tell them that or, in the noise and hubbub of the crowd, no one heard what he was saying, because he was immediately flogged, as was his companion, Silas. Then they were dragged to a jail built into the side of the acropolis. There they were thrown into a filthy dungeon, their backs raw and bleeding, and their feet were fastened in stocks.

A Bad Situation

It was a bad situation for Paul and Silas, probably quite a bit worse than most of us have ever faced. But their attitudes certainly didn't reflect their circumstances. Verse 25 tells us, "About midnight Paul and Silas were praying and singing hymns to God, and the other prisoners were listening to them." Isn't that interesting? At the dark hour of midnight, in a seemingly hopeless situation, they were praying and singing hymns to God. Not only that, *the other prisoners were listening to them.* Have you ever realized that your attitude, the way you behave under adverse circumstances, is not only important to you, it is also important to those around you who may be watching and listening to see how you are going to react?

So there they were, praying and singing, with the other prisoners listening to them, when, "Suddenly there was such a violent earthquake that the foundations of the prison were shaken. At once all the prison doors flew open, and everybody's chains came loose" (v. 26). Now, either Paul and Silas were such bad singers that they caused the earthquake, or God had intervened, setting not only Paul and Silas free, but the other prisoners who had been listening, as well.

A True Awakening

Apparently the jailer had not been listening to their singing, however, because verse 27 tells us that, when the earthquake shook and the chains clanked off onto the ground, "The jailer woke up, and when he saw the prison doors open, he drew his sword and was about to kill himself because he thought the prisoners had escaped." The jailer had been sleeping on the job. It was midnight, he was tired, and he was sure the prisoners were securely locked up for the night, so he had gone to sleep. When he awoke and saw the prison doors open, he was terrified that the prisoners had escaped, and he knew he would be held responsible. He quickly decided it would be better to take his own life than to fall into the hands of the Roman authorities.

But before he could end his life, Paul shouted, "Don't harm yourself! We are all here!" (v. 28). Paul took command of the situation, and the jailer "rushed in and fell trembling before Paul and Silas" (v. 29).

"Sirs, what must I do to be saved?" the jailer asked them.

And they answered, "Believe in the Lord Jesus, and you will be saved—you and your household" (v. 31). And the man was converted, as was his entire family— certainly not the ending that Satan had hoped for when he first launched his attack against Paul and Silas to disrupt their ministry. But their attitude of confidence in God, their dependence and faith in His deliverance, even in the worst circumstances, made all the difference.

Authorities Worried

The next day, when the authorities sent word that Paul and Silas were to be released, Paul refused to leave, saying "They beat us publicly without a trial, even though we are Roman citizens, and threw us into prison. And now do they want to get rid of us quietly? No! Let them come themselves and escort us out" (v. 37).

When the authorities were told that Paul and Silas were Roman citizens, they were very worried and upset. It was a serious offense to flog a Roman citizen. Verse 39 says, "They came to appease them and escorted them from the prison, requesting them to leave the city."

AN ATTITUDE OF REJOICING AND HUMILITY

And so, after a relatively short visit in Philippi, Paul had to move on. But the memory of Philippi was written deeply on his heart, and even though Paul didn't always receive the support he needed from other churches to continue on in his ministry, the believers in Philippi were always faithful in their financial support of him.

Paul appreciated this support and, in his letter to them (probably written from a prison in Rome), he said, "I thank my God every time I remember you. In all my prayers for all of you, I always pray with joy because of your partnership in the gospel from the first day until now" (Phil. 1:3-5). Their support of his ministry made them partners with Paul in the spreading of the gospel, and they had never failed or slacked off in that support.

Paul's letter to the Philippians reflected, once again, his attitude in adversity. He said to them in Philippians 4:4, "Rejoice in the Lord always. I will say it again: Rejoice!" He also told them in the twelfth verse of chapter one, "Now I want you to know, brothers, that what has happened to me has really served to advance the gospel." In other words, he was saying to them, "Don't feel bad for me. Rejoice! What has happened to me—my imprisonment, my physical trials—have brought about the advancement of the gospel." Paul was able to see how God could use even the bad things in life to accomplish His purpose, and Paul was telling the Philippian believers that he wanted them to have that same attitude, the attitude of Christ.

> *Your attitude should be the same as that of Christ Jesus: Who, being in very nature God, did not consider equality with God something to be*

*H*e (Paul) wanted to encourage them to have the right attitudes as believers, attitudes that would affect the way they lived their lives.

grasped, but made himself nothing, taking the very nature of a servant, being made in human likeness. And being found in appearance as a man, he humbled himself and became obedient to death—even death on a cross! (Phil. 2:5-8).

A LETTER ABOUT ATTITUDES

And then, of course, Paul said something that the Philippians would recognize immediately. He said, "Our citizenship is in heaven" (Phil. 3:20). That was important to the Philippians, you see, because they were Roman colonists out in the middle of Macedonia. They thought of Rome as their home. They always thought in terms of Rome being where they belonged. But Paul told them, "You're living on earth, but your citizenship is in heaven. Always bear that in mind." He wanted them to remember that, and to reflect that thought always in their attitudes.

Paul's entire letter to the Philippians was really a letter about attitudes. He wanted to encourage them to have the right attitudes as believers, attitudes that would affect the way they lived their lives and, in turn, affect the lives of those around them who were watching, listening, waiting to see how they would react to circumstances and situations. With an attitude of prayer, an attitude of rejoicing in the Lord always, and an attitude of the humility of Christ, he knew they could triumph, even as he had learned to do.

I can do all things through Christ which strengtheneth me (Phil. 4:13, *KJV*).

SOMETHING TO THINK ABOUT

1. What can you do in your life to establish a more faithful attitude of prayer and of confidence in God? What results can you see happening because of that commitment?

2. How can you maintain an attitude that rejoices in all things? How can you allow the mind of Christ Jesus to also be in you, that you might bear in your body the humility of the very Son of God?

CHAPTER 5

ATHENS

STAYING TRUE TO THE CALL

The Greeks have always prided themselves on their gorgeous, clear blue sky. Although it's still gorgeous and usually blue, unfortunately it's not always clear anymore. The smog, even in the beautiful city of Athens, has taken its toll. Many of the ancient monuments that have withstood all kinds of wars and fighting are now actually crumbling as a result of pollution.

But that's modern Athens, and right now we're concerned with ancient Athens, that splendid architectural delight to which the apostle Paul came, an artistic, aesthetic city. Of course, even then, there were many things wrong with Athens, as Paul quickly discovered. But before we get into that, let's talk a little bit about how Paul happened to arrive in this center of culture, Athens.

MOVING TOWARD ATHENS

Paul had been traveling in many different areas preaching Christ. He had been in Asia Minor; he had tried to go into several different places, but the Spirit had not allowed him to; and then he had the vision of the man of Macedonia. Promptly, he got on a boat and headed to Neapolis, trekked up the Via Ignacia, over the winding hills and steep precipitous mountainsides, until he came into the magnificent city of Philippi. Although he wasn't able to stay there long, he was there long enough to plant a church.

From there Paul went to Thessalonica, where he started another church. It wasn't long, however, before he ran into trouble again when some jealous Jews organized a mob and started a riot (see Acts 17:5-9), and so he moved on to a little place called Berea, where he was warmly received by the people in the synagogue. In Acts 17:11, these Bereans were referred to as being of "more noble character than the Thessalonians, for they received the message with great eagerness and examined the Scriptures every day to see if what Paul said was true."

Searching the Scriptures

Isn't that interesting? The Bereans were considered noble because, when they heard the gospel message, they not only received it with eagerness, they searched the Scriptures to see if the message was true. What an important thing that is for us to remember! When some new message or idea comes along, do we accept it blindly? Or are we willing to take the time to examine the Scriptures to see if that message, that idea, lines up with God's Word? I believe if we would learn to faithfully take the time to

A view of the Acropolis from Mars Hill. (Photo © Joyce Thimsen)

search the Scriptures before jumping into things, we would save ourselves a lot of heartache and grief and backtracking.

Berea was a bit of a haven for Paul, but he wasn't able to stay there very long either, because some rough characters came down to Berea from Thessalonica and made things so difficult for him that he was forced to move on. Boarding a ship, he sailed down the rugged coastline until he eventually came to Athens.

DOING WHAT HE DID BEST

Now, Paul was not unmindful of Greek literature, nor was he unconcerned about beauty. Undoubtedly, he was impressed by some of the things he saw when he arrived in Athens. Anyone who has ever been to Athens and had the opportunity of seeing the Parthenon, for example, of hearing about its intricate design and the incredible mathematical calculations that went into that building, cannot help but be impressed. During Paul's stay in Athens, the superlative art forms of those ancient Greeks were on display wherever the Apostle went throughout the city. It would have been impossible for Paul not to have been aware of the sheer human skill that had gone into the development of the city. But, in spite of all this, Paul was deeply troubled.

Acts 17:16 says "While Paul was waiting for them [Silas and Timothy] in Athens, he was greatly distressed to see that the city was full of idols." Besides that, he was lonely and discouraged. His heart was with the infant churches that he had planted, wondering how they were doing, wishing he could be with them to encourage them. Paul felt toward those churches the way parents feel toward their children. In 1 Thessalonians 2:7, Paul likened his relationship with the infant church in Thessalonica to that of "a mother caring for her little children." In verse 11, he went on to say, "For you know that we dealt with each of you as a father deals with his own children."

So, there he was, all alone in a big city, concerned about the churches he had left behind, and distressed by the idolatry he saw all around him. What did he do? He decided to do what he did best. He began to proclaim the gospel. "So he reasoned in the synagogue with the Jews and the God-fearing Greeks, as well as in the marketplace day by day with those who happened to be there" (Acts 17:17).

When in Greece . . .

One of the great things about the apostle Paul was that he had learned, when he ministered, to be all things to all men (see 1 Cor. 9:22). In other words, he had learned to adapt to his surroundings, to use different techniques of communicating to different people. In Athens, a city given over to philosophy, he entered into debates and discussions with the Athenians. There was nothing they liked better than to hear some new philosophy presented so that they could argue, debate and discuss it. Acts 17:21 tells us, "(All the Athenians and the foreigners who lived there spent their time doing nothing but talking about and listening to the latest ideas)."

The marketplace, or agora, was a favorite place for the Athenians to gather for discussion and debate, so Paul made use of this custom, walking along the shady areas of the marketplace, standing under the canopies of the various stores, proclaiming to any who would listen that Jesus had risen from the dead. Word got out about this strange man who had come with these new ideas, and soon he was summoned to meet with a group of people known as the

*E*verything he (Paul) told them about God was in direct contrast to all they believed.

Areopagites. They met on a place called Areopagus or Mars Hill, a fascinating outcrop of rock and a rather precarious place to stand.

Reasoning with the Philosophers

The Areopagites were a community of brilliant, philosophical people who evaluated and judged people either on the basis of what they had done, or on the basis of what they had said. Possibly they were some sort of a criminal court, or perhaps just a philosophical forum. There was a special stone upon which the person who was defending either his actions or his position would stand. Paul was placed on that stone, and all the philosophers sat around, ready to hear what he had to say.

These people had called Paul a babbler (see Acts 17:18), but the word they used actually means *seed picker,* indicating that they felt he had no ideas of his own, that he was like a sparrow, jumping around, picking up other people's seeds or ideas. But Paul soon introduced to them some entirely new ideas and concepts that they had never heard before.

Paul impressed them by immediately quoting some of their ancient classical writers. He reminded them that one of their own writers had said that it is "in him [God] we live and move and have our being," and that "we are his offspring" (v. 28). He then pointed out to them a strange anomaly. He said, "Men of Athens! I see that in every way you are very religious. For as I walked around and looked carefully at your objects of worship, I even found an altar with this inscription: TO AN UNKNOWN GOD" (vv. 22,23). Then, at the end of verse 23, Paul made a very powerful statement: "Now what you worship as something unknown I am going to proclaim to you."

It is important to remember at this point that Paul was

standing in the shadow of the Parthenon, the place where it was acknowledged that there were innumerable gods. The gods of ancient Greece were a strange amalgam of gods, gods who were believed to possess phenomenal powers, as well as the worst of human vices. And here was Paul, boldly declaring to these people the only true and living God. Everything he told them about God was in direct contrast to all they believed about the gods they worshiped. In essence, he told them that God is the One who made the universe, who made all things, the One in whom we live and move and have our being, the One who must be worshiped for who He is (see vv. 24-28).

Now, the problem with the Greeks was that they were starting with themselves, using their own ingenuity and imagination to manufacture their own gods. Paul was saying to them, No, we don't start with ourselves, however ingenious we might be; we start with God revealing Himself to us. And that, of course, is fundamental to the Christian faith. Christianity is not the product of human philosophy; it is the result of divine revelation.

THE IMPORTANCE OF THE RESURRECTION

Paul then went on to say that this God who had revealed Himself is a God who always requires us to live and behave in certain ways. He told those skeptical, cynical philosophers sitting around him that God was not at all impressed with the way they were living. And then, he made a very brave, courageous, powerful statement. He declared that this God who had revealed Himself, this God who was far removed from all the gods of the Greek Parthenon, this God is the God who will judge all men. And then he said that this very God had already appointed

Christianity stands or falls on whether or not Jesus rose from the dead.

the Judge, and that He had raised this Judge from the dead.

> For he has set a day when he will judge the world with justice by this man he has appointed. He has given proof of this to all men by raising him from the dead (Acts 17:31).

Getting Their Attention

That did it. As soon as the apostle Paul began to talk about raising somebody from the dead, he really had their attention. Some of them were fascinated, while others laughed and mocked him. Things are still pretty much that way, aren't they? You can talk about Jesus as a babe in a manger, you can talk about His being a good man, you can even talk about His hanging on the cross, but when you start to talk about His being raised from the dead, that's when you're going to get some real reaction. Christianity stands or falls on whether or not Jesus rose from the dead. No matter where he was or what the circumstances, Paul always got around to the subject of the Resurrection, because that was the basis of his entire message, the fundamental aspect of Christian truth and Christian theology: either Jesus Christ is risen, or He isn't.

Paul stressed that very point in his first letter to the Corinthians, when he said, "If Christ has not been raised, our preaching is useless and so is your faith" (15:14). On the other hand, he went on to explain, if Christ has risen from the dead, it is the most powerful, wonderful truth imaginable. Not only does that mean that God has revealed Himself; it also means that He loved us enough to give His Son to die for us, that Christ's atoning death was acceptable to God, and that we can have absolute assurance of forgiveness of sins. And, if Christ has been raised from the dead, we shall be raised, also (see vv. 20-22).

A New Course of Action

As if that weren't enough, Paul then went on to tell them what it was that God required of them. "He commands all people everywhere to repent" (Acts 17:30). Now, repentance literally means to change one's mind. Not just a casual change of mind, however; it means an entire change of intent and a whole new course of action. The course of action as a Christian, of course, is simply the action that says, If Jesus Christ is Lord, He shall be my Lord; if Jesus Christ died for sin and I'm one of those sinners for whom He died, then I must turn from my sin and submit my life gladly and joyfully to Him and to His service.

This was the thrust of the sermon that Paul preached up on the Areopagus. He didn't meet with resounding success. There were a few who were converted to Christ, but you won't find any account of a church being established in Athens. We have no epistle to the Athenians because this was one of the areas where the Apostle did not see much response to his message. In fact, shortly after his time with the Areopagites, he moved on from Athens and went down to Corinth, where he tackled another monumental task.

True Discipleship

What a remarkable man Paul was! What a committed man to the gospel of Jesus Christ! It didn't matter whether he was being beaten in Philippi, on the verge of being shipwrecked, going hungry or being abused by his fellow countrymen, we still see his tenacity, his courage, his commitment. We see a man who was absolutely sold out to honoring Christ and to making the good news known. That's true discipleship. And that's what we are supposed to be producing in our churches today.

SOMETHING TO THINK ABOUT

1. When you find yourself in a strange environment, possibly alone and out of your element, what is your reaction? Do you, like Paul, do what you do best? For Paul, that meant to preach the gospel. What does it mean for you?

2. When the pressure is on, how do you go about bringing up the heart of the gospel, the crux of the message, the one thing that you know will get a reaction? Are you willing to publicly declare the reality of the Resurrection, whatever the consequences, or do you look for an easy out, an excuse to avoid a confrontation?

CHAPTER 6

CRETE

WEATHERING THE STORM

Paul's ministry in the major cities such as Corinth, Ephesus and Athens is explained for us in some detail in the New Testament; however, Paul also ministered extensively in other areas, as well, although the Scriptures say very little about those times.

We do know, for instance, that Paul worked on the Mediterranean island of Crete with Titus. During his stay on that island, so much was accomplished that, when it came time for Paul to leave Crete, it was necessary for him to leave Titus behind to oversee things and to appoint elders in every town. This suggests that their ministry on Crete had been far-reaching, and that they had effectively planted churches in many areas of the island.

The island of Crete is dominated by harsh mountains rising out of the sea. It has an area of 3,190 square miles,

with a current population of just over one-half million people. Crete came under the rule of the Romans in 67 B.C., and was still under Roman rule when Paul arrived there. The Romans lost control of Crete to Byzantium in A.D. 395, then the Arabs gained partial control after 824; in 1204, the Venetians took possession. The Venetians were defeated by the Ottoman Turks, who were already in control of part of Crete, in 1669. Finally, in 1898, the Turks were expelled from the island and, in 1913, Crete was united with Greece.[1]

It would be wrong for us to assume that Crete was a primitive little island. In reality, it was the home of one of the world's most remarkable ancient civilizations. The ruins of the palace of Knossos and the discoveries made by archaeologists show that the Cretans to whom Paul ministered were skillful and sophisticated, yet spiritually dead, nevertheless. This is a powerful reminder to us today that even the most inventive and creative people need to be told of Christ, and even the most sociable and sophisticated must be brought to repentance and faith in Him.

NOW THAT I HAVE YOUR ATTENTION

Paul sailed the Mediterranean Sea around and beyond the island of Crete several times. Unfortunately, not all of his trips were enjoyable ones. For instance, in chapter 27 of Acts, we read that Paul had appealed to Caesar and was being shipped off to Rome. They were docked in a harbor in Crete called Fair Havens, near the town of Lasea. Winter was approaching, and Fair Havens was an unsuitable place to stay the winter. The pilot and the owner of the

The harbor of Fair Havens as seen from the hills of the Island of Crete. (Photo © Gilbert Beers)

*T*here he (Paul) was, hanging on to what was left of the ship . . . and suddenly he tells them all to cheer up!

ship were anxious to sail on, but Paul warned them, "Men, I can see that our voyage is going to be disastrous and bring great loss to ship and cargo, and to our own lives also" (v. 10).

But Julius, the centurion in charge of Paul and the other prisoners, thought Paul was trying to put off going to Rome for personal reasons, so, "instead of listening to what Paul said, [the centurion] followed the advice of the pilot and of the owner of the ship" (v. 11).

So, off they went. Before long, a storm arose, and the graphic narrative that the Scriptures give us in Acts 27:13-44 is well worth reading. (In fact, I've heard some people say that it is one of the most magnificent pieces of narrative concerning storms to be found in all of literature.) Anyway, things went from bad to worse for Paul and his shipmates; they didn't see the sun, they didn't see the stars, they didn't know where they were. In the end, they were at the mercy of the wind, driven this way and that, not knowing which way to go.

Then things really got serious, because there was a mutiny on board. The soldiers drew their swords to try to control the sailors. Soon, they were throwing things overboard and cutting loose the lifeboat in order to prevent the crew from escaping. In the midst of all this chaos, where anarchy was threatening to take over, a very interesting thing happened. The apostle Paul appeared on deck. He was probably staggering, trying desperately to maintain a foothold and to be heard above the raging wind and seas. What had he come on deck to say to the others?

I like the way it says it in the King James Version best: "Be of good cheer" (v. 22). Isn't that just what you'd expect from Paul? There he was, hanging on to what was left of the ship as it rolled and tossed and disintegrated beneath him, everyone around him in panic, the crew threatening to riot, and suddenly he tells them all to cheer up! Paul wasn't just some dull, dry theologian, was he? He was a man who lived his faith. He practiced what he preached! He was a man who actually could stand on a sinking ship and tell an almost hysterical mob to cheer up. That's faith.

PAUL'S PHILOSOPHY

Once he had their attention—and believe me, his advice to cheer up was so radical it definitely got everyone's attention—he then went about getting them organized. First, he told them that God had assured him they were all going to survive (see v. 24). Then, he proclaimed his faith in God's promise by adding, "I have faith in God that it will happen just as he told me" (v. 25). Although the ship was eventually lost, God kept His promise, and all 276 people on board made it safely to shore.

I believe it was Paul's philosophy, "To live is Christ and to die is gain" (Phil. 1:21), that was going through his mind all the time he was on that sinking ship. In fact, that same thought was probably what kept him going on many occasions, especially when he was locked up in that dingy cell in a Philippian jail. With that thought in mind, he was able to sing praises to God, in spite of a bleeding back and stocks on his feet. Without that philosophy, how could he possibly praise God under those dark and dismal circumstances?

And then, after the earthquake came and loosed the prisoners and opened the prison doors, Paul was concerned with the jailer who was about to commit suicide because he thought the prisoners had escaped. He intervened, stopped the jailer from killing himself, and led him to Christ. I like that about Paul, don't you? It didn't matter whether he was on a sinking ship trying to cheer people up, or singing hymns that brought on an earthquake and caused a man to come to Christ, he was demonstrating his philosophy, "to live is Christ and to die is gain."

A Concern for Others

There are many more instances of how the apostle Paul handled these difficult circumstances, but let me just talk about one in particular. Once again, we find Paul in prison and, with his wrists and ankles in chains, he is dragged in before King Agrippa. Dirty, disheveled, dressed in rough prison garb, he is suddenly thrust into this magnificent room with the king and queen sitting on their thrones and all the nobility surrounding them. True to form, Paul says, "King Agrippa, I consider myself fortunate to stand before you today" (Acts 26:2). In essence, Paul was saying, "I'm really happy to be here." Now, I realize that's the way all good preachers begin their sermons, but these were not normal circumstances. Paul truly meant what he said; he was glad to be there, glad to have a chance to speak to the people gathered there that day.

The king and queen and all the others in the room, of course, were there to hear Paul defend his position concerning Christianity. And so, Paul begins by defending his own experience (see vv. 2-23). Nobody could refute that. But he wasn't satisfied with that because, like all good preachers, he knew that the people were listening to him. He could sense that he was getting through to them. So he began to press on with what he was saying. He walked up to King Agrippa and asked the king if he believed what he (Paul) had been saying (see v. 27). Before the king could answer, Paul said, "I know you do" (v. 27).

At that point, King Agrippa made one of the most memorable and possibly one of the most tragic statements found in the Bible: "Almost thou persuadest me to be a Christian" (v. 28, *KJV*).

What was Paul's response to that statement? "I pray God that not only you but all who are listening to me today may become what I am" (v. 29). Paul's concern was not to convince the king to grant him his freedom; he was not even thinking about himself or his chains. He was thinking of those who were listening to him, those people who sat there in their regal finery and false sense of security, those people who were the real prisoners because they had not found freedom in Christ. His heart cry was that they might believe his message and receive the gospel and come to a saving knowledge of Christ.

Unfortunately, that wasn't the case. Verses 30 and 31 tell us, "The king rose, and with him the governor and Bernice [the queen] and those sitting with them. They left the room." How tragic. They had their chance, they heard the truth, but they turned their backs and walked away. There is no further account anywhere in the Bible that tells us that the king or any of those who sat in that room listening to Paul that day ever had another chance to accept Christ.

To Live or to Die

But, in spite of their indifference to his message, their rejection of the gospel, Paul remained true to his calling. He did not back down in the face of adversity. He did not compromise or plead for his freedom. Instead, he moved into a bad situation, took charge, counted himself fortunate to be there, and came across with a powerful proclamation of Christ. Once again, his philosophy, "To live is Christ and to die is gain," kept him true, kept him faithful.

You know, there are actually only two things we need to do as human beings: we need to learn to live, and we

*W*herever he went . . . Paul
held on to the thought
that Christ . . . keeps what is
committed to Him.

need to learn to die. I've often told people that and they think I'm kidding at first, but I'm serious. Think about it. We complicate matters, but it really couldn't be much more basic than that. And that's exactly what Paul was saying when he said, "To live is Christ and to die is gain." He was so utterly convinced of who Christ is that he was prepared to commit himself completely to God's call on his life. Wherever he went, whether on a sinking ship, standing before a king or sitting in a prison at midnight, Paul held on to the thought that his life was committed to Christ, and that Christ keeps what is committed to Him.

Paul knew that Jesus Christ had committed His life to him; therefore, in Christ he had all the resources he would ever need to do what God had called him to do. Because of that, he thought in terms of Christ being his life at all times. If the ship is sinking, he thought, I will either live or die, but if I go on living, then Christ will be all I need. But if I die, then that will be to my advantage. Standing in front of King Agrippa, knowing all the time that the king could do away with him, Paul reasoned that if the king did decide to have him executed, then he would die. If not, he would go on living, and Christ was his life.

So what did Paul mean when he said, "To die is gain"? He meant that, as he lived his life, he enjoyed all that Christ is, but he also got beaten, shipwrecked, thrown into prison, and had to face all sorts of difficult circumstances. Nevertheless, he knew Christ was all he needed to get through. But, if he were to die, then he knew he would still have Christ, just as he had while he lived; but he would no longer have to endure the beatings, prison, times of hunger, loneliness, and all the other heartaches and difficulties that were a part of his life. That is why he could say, If I can enjoy Christ now, with all I have to endure while I am alive, how wonderful it will be when I can enjoy Christ without all those things! Therefore, Christ is my life, and death is my gain.

A famous quote from William Shakespeare, "To be or not to be, that is the question," reflects the torturous indecision of one suspended between the fear of dying and the agony of living. In essence, Paul said the same thing— to be or not to be. But his attitude was one of hope, rather than despair. If I go on living, he said, Christ is my life, but if I don't go on living, death is my gain. You just can't knock a man down who lives with that philosophy.

SOMETHING TO THINK ABOUT

1. What is the heart of your philosophy? If you're not sure, think back to the worst trials of your life. Now, what thought(s) did you cling to to get you through? Where did the sufficiency of Christ fit into those thoughts?

2. What is the worst possible situation in which you can imagine yourself? How can you know that, if you are committed to Christ, He will keep that which is committed to Him and see you through that situation? How does your faith line up with Job's, who said, "Though he slay me, yet will I trust in him" (Job 13:15, *KJV*)? Or with Paul's faith, which enabled him to say, "For to me, to live is Christ and to die is gain" (Phil. 1:21)?

SECTION THREE
COST OF BEING A DISCIPLE

CHAPTER 7

JERUSALEM

REPENTANCE, SUBMISSION AND SURRENDER

L ocated near the center of Israel is the beautiful old city of Jerusalem, declared by the state of Israel to be its capital since Israel won the Six-Day War in June 1967. Because of its high altitude and lack of heavy industry, Jerusalem has not yet been faced with any serious problems of air pollution.

The city has, however, been the site of seemingly endless wars and fighting, primarily because it is considered to be one of the principal holy places not only of Judaism and Christianity, but Islam, as well. After the Arab-Israeli War of 1948, Jerusalem was divided between Transjordan (later known as Jordan), which annexed the part of Jerusalem known as the Old City, along with the rest of East Jerusalem; and Israel, which held West Jerusalem. After Israel captured East Jerusalem in the 1967 war, the entire

Just beyond the Dome of the Rock, which sits on the old Temple site, lies the city of Jerusalem. In the foreground, just above the Garden of Gethsemane, is the church of Mary Magdalene. (Photo © Gilbert Beers)

city of Jerusalem was declared to be Israel's eternal and indivisible capital. The Arab neighbors of the new Jewish state have never accepted this, and so the status of the city has become a major point of contention between them.[1]

A SIMPLE, BASIC VISION

On the north side of the ancient city of Jerusalem is the Damascus Gate. It was through this gate that the apostle Paul (then known as Saul of Tarsus) left Jerusalem in a fury against the followers of Jesus who were living in that city and had spread out into other areas, as well.

Saul had taken it upon himself to exterminate the followers of the Way (as the Christians were then known), and he was seeking permission to go to Damascus so that he could bring his own special brand of hatred to bear against them. As he made his way through the crowds out the Damascus Gate, pushing his way north, he proceeded along the old Roman road winding through the hills, enduring the heat and the dust, as the intensity of his antagonism built up within him. Suddenly, a very dramatic thing happened. Saul had a vision. It was a very simple, very basic vision. The vision that he had was a vision of the risen Christ.

THE ESSENCE OF REPENTANCE

You see, the problem that Saul of Tarsus had was that he was totally convinced that he was right and that Jesus of Nazareth was wrong. Saul was totally convinced that when Jesus died and was buried, that was the end of it. All of those pernicious rumors that Jesus was risen from the dead only added to the depth and intensity of Saul's own

*T*his powerful witness of the dying martyr Stephen hit home in the hardened heart of Saul of Tarsus, leaving a question mark that was difficult for him to ignore.

convictions. To be confronted with a vision of the risen Christ showed him something that he did not want to see. Number one, it showed him that he was wrong; number two, it showed him that Jesus was right, a total reversal of all that he had believed.

And that's the essence of repentance. Repentance means to change one's mind. Initially, we all think we are right and that Jesus is wrong. When we come to the point of repentance, we change our minds. We admit that Jesus is the One who is right and that we are the ones who have been wrong all along. The result of this revelation of Jesus Christ should be the same for us as it was for Saul: we should fall at His feet as Saul did and ask, "Lord, what wilt thou have me to do?" (Acts 9:6, *KJV*). That response from Saul was a great act of submission. It was also a tremendous act of surrender. It was the attitude that was to stay with him for the rest of his life.

BEING PREPARED FOR THE VISION

Of course, this event didn't just happen right out of the blue. Prior to Saul's going through the Damascus Gate on his quest to persecute the followers of the Way, he had another very interesting experience. Along the wall of Jerusalem is a gate known as Saint Stephen's Gate. It was there that an event of great significance took place, an event that had far-reaching effects on Saul of Tarsus.

A Powerful Witness

You see, Stephen, one of those seven men chosen by the apostles to look after the affairs of the widows of the church of Jerusalem, had, along with Philip and the others, dealt with all those affairs, and then gotten on with the business of witnessing. Stephen had become so powerful and so effective in his witnessing and so winsome in his ways that he was challenged by the authorities. He was hauled in front of the Sanhedrin (the highest ruling Jewish court of that day) and required to give his defense. His defense moved into a powerful evangelistic sermon, including a tremendous survey of the history of Israel and leading up to the proof that Jesus was indeed the Messiah (see Acts 7:2-53).

All of this that Stephen had to say was not what those listening wanted to hear. People who have closed their minds to the truth are usually like that. They will listen to you as long as you tell them what they want to hear. When you tell them anything else, no matter how eloquently or persuasively you might say it, they will either ignore you or, as was the case with those listening to Stephen, they will react in anger. Acts 7:54 tells us about those listening to Stephen: "When they heard this, they were furious and gnashed their teeth at him." They weren't just a little upset; they were furious. When you start gnashing your teeth, you are just about as angry as you can ever get.

So, there was Stephen, with his face shining like that of an angel (see Acts 6:15), standing in front of this furious mob, and what does he do then? Acts 7:55 says, "But Stephen, full of the Holy Spirit, looked up to heaven and saw the glory of God, and Jesus standing at the right hand of God." And then he said, "Look . . . I see the heaven open and the Son of Man standing at the right hand of God" (v. 56).

Well, that did it. They could stand to hear no more. Stephen was rushed out of the place, taken to what is now called Saint Stephen's Gate and stoned. One man who stood watching Stephen's execution was Saul of Tarsus. The Bible gives us this account:

A vision of the risen Christ showed him (Saul) . . . a total reversal of all that he had believed. And that's the essence of repentance.

At this they covered their ears and, yelling at the top of their voices, they all rushed at him, dragged him out of the city and began to stone him. Meanwhile, the witnesses laid their clothes at the feet of a young man named Saul (vv. 57,58).

A Question Mark

The most telling statement about Saul of Tarsus is found at the end of verse 60: "And Saul was there, giving approval to his death." Now, it wasn't just that this young man Stephen died, it was the way he died that had to have had an effect on Saul, in spite of the fact that Saul stood watching and approving the death of Stephen. For, as Stephen died, he knelt down and, while those involved in his death looked on, he said, "Lord, do not hold this sin against them" (7:60). His words were remarkably reminiscent of our Lord's words as He hung on the cross: "Father, forgive them, for they do not know what they are doing" (Luke 23:34).

This powerful witness of the dying martyr Stephen hit home in the hardened heart of Saul of Tarsus, leaving a question mark that was difficult for him to ignore. Even though he continued to persecute believers with zeal, his heart was being prepared, tenderized by the work of the Holy Spirit and through the witness of believers. Then, when the revelation of the risen Christ appeared to him, Saul had no alternative but to face up to the fact that Jesus Christ is Lord, acknowledge that fact, and then submit himself to His service.

EAGER TO PAY THE DEBT

Years later, writing to the Romans, the apostle Paul showed that he clearly grasped the immensity of the commission our Lord gave to His disciples on the Mount of Olives (see Acts 1:8). Paul said, "I am not ashamed of the gospel, because it is the power of God for the salvation of everyone who believes" (Rom. 1:16). He also said, "I am obligated both to Greeks and non-Greeks, both to the wise and the foolish" (v. 14). In other words, it didn't matter who people were; he was in their debt to proclaim to them the risen, living Christ. Not only was he in their debt to proclaim the gospel, he was anxious to do so, as he stated in verse 15: "That is why I am so eager to preach the gospel also to you who are at Rome."

We need to grab on to these words of Paul. We need to make them a part of us. We must not only recognize our duty, our debt to proclaim the gospel message to all people, regardless of race, nationality or social standing; we must do so out of an eager heart. We will only be able to do that when we, like Saul of Tarsus on the Damascus Road, catch a vision of the risen Christ, repent, and fall at His feet in submission and surrender, asking, "Lord, what wilt thou have me to do?"

SOMETHING TO THINK ABOUT

1. When did you walk the Damascus Road? How did that walk lead to your acknowledgment that Jesus Christ is right, leaving you with the obvious conclusion that you were wrong? How did that time of repentance affect you? Did it cause you to throw yourself at the feet of our Lord in submission and surrender, asking Him what He would have you do in service to Him? What was His answer to you at that point?

2. Now that you've repented, submitted and surrendered

yourself to Christ, how have you dealt with the realization of your debt to declare the gospel to any and all who would listen? Is it possible to kindle a burning desire and eagerness to do just that? If so, how?

CHAPTER 8

SHILOH
YIELDING AND PRODUCING

A s we visit the ancient site of Shiloh, we will be discussing the very tender subject of yielding to God's will, as well as bearing and producing fruit. Foregoing our own will and yielding to that of God's will for our lives is not an easy thing for any of us. A classic example of a yielded life was that of a very special lady from the Old Testament, Hannah. Because my wife, Jill, feels a certain kinship and empathy for Hannah, I would like her to take over at this point and tell you about Hannah's relationship with God.

A YIELDED HEART

Yes is the language of relinquishment, the language of a yielded heart, whether spoken by the martyrs in the Colosseum, the apostles in far-off lands or humble women in

The remains of a watchtower stands in the Shiloh area.
(Photo © Gilbert Beers)

Yes is the language of relinquishment, the language of a yielded heart.

bygone centuries. Hannah knew how to say yes. I pray that, as we study Hannah's yielded life, we too will find ourselves saying yes to God.

Shiloh was a Canaanite town, a central sanctuary site for the Israelites during the twelfth and eleventh centuries B.C. Shiloh was also the place where the Tabernacle and the Ark of the Covenant were kept until the Philistines captured the Ark around 1050 B.C. Not long after that, Shiloh was destroyed.[1]

Giving Up Our Children

It was in the town of Shiloh where Hannah, one of my favorite ladies, brought her little boy, Samuel, and literally gave him into the hands of others to raise. Now, Hannah is one of my favorite ladies for many reasons. I suppose one of the most obvious reasons is that she and I are both mothers. As a mother, I know how difficult it is to give up your children.

I remember what it was like when our oldest child left for college. I would sit at the kitchen table, sipping my cup of coffee and thinking of all the walks I didn't take him on, all the stories I didn't read him, and how hard it was for me to let him go.

That's why it intrigues me that this lovely lady, Hannah, could bring her small son into that place in ancient times and give him into the hands of evil men. Because, even though there was a temple there, even though the old Tabernacle had been placed in Shiloh, the priests who were ministering there, Eli and his two sons, Hophni and Phinehas, were not godly men. But in spite of the fact that they were not godly men, little Samuel was supposed to be trained by them to love God. How did this situation ever come about?

Praying in Bitterness of Soul

In Hannah's day, it was not unusual for a man to have more than one wife. Hannah had to share her husband, Elkanah, with another woman, a woman who disapproved of Hannah. The other woman, Peninnah, had given Elkanah children; but Hannah was barren, which not only distressed Hannah, it confused her. In those days, childbearing was equated with God's blessing and favor, while barrenness was equated with God's disfavor. Hannah undoubtedly anguished over what it was that she had done to incur God's disfavor.

Hannah wanted a baby desperately. Each year, year after year, she would go faithfully to the temple and pray to God to give her a child. Her rival, Peninnah, knew how badly Hannah wanted a child, and she chided her unmercifully, until Hannah would end up in tears. Although Elkanah tried to console Hannah, nothing could take away the emptiness inside her, that aching and longing to hold her own baby in her arms. And so she continued to pray. But God did not answer her prayers.

Have you ever wondered why God doesn't seem to answer certain prayers? I've often wondered that. Prayer is such a difficult thing to get a handle on. It seems so easy, and yet it can be so difficult, especially when the sky seems like brass and you feel as if no one is listening.

Hannah felt like that. It says here in 1 Samuel 1:10 that Hannah was in "bitterness of soul," and that she "wept much and prayed to the Lord." She was so heartbroken and bitter that she couldn't eat. It was affecting her health to the point that Elkanah came to her and said, "Hannah, why are you weeping? Why don't you eat? Why are you downhearted? Don't I mean more to you than ten sons?" (v. 8).

You know what the answer to that was? No, buddy, you don't! Elkanah meant well, but he was the sort of man who didn't quite understand his wife, even though he obviously loved her dearly. Sometimes, even our husbands don't understand us, particularly when it concerns something that only a woman can really understand, like wanting babies. How can men ever really understand that? So, Hannah wasn't able to share with her husband the thing that was really troubling her.

Well, she believed in God. Why didn't she share it with Him? She did. She went into the temple and prayed to God in bitterness of soul. She had a hurting heart. Have you ever had a hurting heart? Do you have a hurting heart now? Have you ever prayed to God, imploring Him from the bitterness of your heart, God, hear my prayer! Hannah prayed like that, promising Him that, if He would give her a son, she would dedicate his life to the service of the Lord (see v. 11).

And, as she prayed, old Eli the priest was sitting there by the temple, watching this woman in prayer, grieving and crying, and he thought she was drunk! That's how far out of touch with God Eli was. He couldn't even distinguish a hurting, grieving, praying woman from a drunkard.

When Eli saw her, he said to her, "How long will you keep on getting drunk? Get rid of your wine" (v. 14).

But Hannah answered him, "Not so, my lord, . . . I am a woman who is deeply troubled" (v. 15).

And then Eli said in verse 17, "Go in peace, and may the God of Israel grant you what you have asked of him."

Letting Go

That was all she needed. Verse 18 tells us, "Then she went her way and ate something, and her face was no longer downcast." What I believe happened to Hannah at that very moment was that she gave up that thing that meant more to her than life itself. There comes a point in prayer where you have to give up. What is it that you want so much? Is it possible for you to come to God and say, Your will, not mine, be done? Because, when Hannah came to that point, she was finally able to say, All right, God, if I have a baby, he shall be yours and serve you forever. But if I don't have a baby, that's all right, too. I'm letting go.

I've had that very experience in my own life. I remember, when my husband was an evangelist and was away from home for ten months out of the year, I would pray to God over and over again, Lord, let my husband stay home! For ten years, I felt, in a sense, as though I didn't have a husband and my children didn't have a father. For a short while, I was like Hannah, begging and imploring God to let my husband stay home with us. And I was like Hannah in that I had a hurting heart, even though I believed in God. I was a missionary, I was serving God, but God just wasn't hearing or answering my prayers. It wasn't until I gave up, really gave up, like Hannah did, that the peace came; when I was finally able to say, All right, your will, Lord, not mine; if he has to be away doing your work for the rest of his life, it's all right.

You know, the story of Hannah is an amazing one. She had a child and named him Samuel, which means "God heard." Can you imagine what that baby meant to Hannah after waiting and praying for all those years? But when he was born, she knew she had to honor her promise to God and give up Samuel to be raised by the priests so that he might serve God all his life. And so, once Samuel was weaned, she gave him up.

Sometimes you have to give up the idea, the prayer, the want, the desire, and sometimes you even have to give up a person—a child, as Hannah did, or a husband, as I did. But the most thrilling thing about this story of Hannah is the fact that after Hannah had come to the temple and given Samuel into the hands of the priests, she wrote a song. It's the song that Mary, the mother of Jesus, borrowed. We call Mary's song the Magnificat, and it's found in the Gospel of Luke, chapter 1, verses 46-55.

Rejoicing in God

In the first line of Hannah's song, she says, "My heart rejoices in the LORD" (1 Sam. 2:1). That's what happens when you give up everything to God—your hopes, your dreams, your desires—and say, Your will, God, not mine. God gives you a rejoicing heart, a laughing heart. Do you have a laughing heart? Wouldn't you like to have a laughing heart instead of a hurting heart? Wouldn't you like to say, My heart rejoices in the Lord and not in circumstances? That's what Hannah was able to say, even after giving up little Samuel.

I remember the first time I really gave up demanding of God that He answer my prayer and leave my husband home with me. The next time I took Stuart to the airport and saw him off for another three months, I turned around to come home and suddenly found that I had a laughing heart! I had never had a laughing heart under those circumstances before. But, like Hannah, my heart was rejoicing in my Lord, and not in my circumstances. And, even though I had three long months to wait before I saw my husband again, I was able to say, God, you're the giver of laughter and of life! I could say that because I had joy and abundant life in Christ to make up for the time I did not have that man of mine whom I love so very much.

Hannah found God to be the giver of laughter and the giver of abundant life because, after she gave up Samuel,

God gave Hannah other children. She didn't even know she was going to have other children when she gave up Samuel, but she kept her vow to God, and He blessed her.

What happened to Samuel? Well, little Samuel grew up to be a prophet, a teacher and a mighty leader of Israel. Everyone heard about him from Dan to Beer-sheba, from one end of the country to the other. And, through Samuel, God's voice was heard once again throughout the land as Samuel began to faithfully instruct Israel in the ways of the Lord. How proud Hannah must have been—but it did not happen without sacrifice.

PRODUCING GOOD FRUIT

Hannah's sacrifice isn't the only thing for which the ancient site of Shiloh is noted. As I said earlier, Shiloh was a central sanctuary site for the Israelites. When you think of the word sanctuary, you think of a place of refuge or protection. The only way anyone could truly feel secure in a place of sanctuary would be to know that someone is watching out for any signs of approaching danger. And that's why, at Shiloh as well as other ancient sites, we find the remains of old watchtowers. A watchtower enabled the inhabitants of a particular area to be alerted to any possible problems or dangers because the watchman, from his lofty perch, could see far off into the distance, spotting trouble before it arrived.

The Lord of the Vineyard

The old prophet Isaiah had a lot to say about watchtowers. He wrote a song in chapter 5, telling about a watchtower. He used it to paint a picture, an illustration of the care of Jehovah for His people. The story in Isaiah 5 tells us that Jehovah had a vineyard on a very fruitful hill, that He dug it and gathered out all the stones, then planted it with the choicest vines. In the middle of it, He built a watchtower (see vv. 1,2). At the bottom of the watchtower was a room, and at the top was a lookout chamber so that the keeper of the vineyard could watch for approaching enemies.

Isaiah's illustration is indeed a wonderful picture of God's care for His people. God takes every precaution, spares no time or effort, to insure that His vineyard produces good fruit. But verse 2 goes on to tell us that, "He looked for a crop of good grapes, but it yielded only bad fruit."

The Vineyards of Our Lives

Isn't that a lot like the vineyards of our lives? Do you ever feel that God has hedged you in, watched over you, done everything possible for you? He has, you know. Do you appreciate it? Do you thank Him for it, or do you mumble and complain and feel sorry for yourself, returning to God nothing more than sour grapes and bad fruit?

If you live in the Western world and you're fortunate enough to be healthy, well fed and clothed, God has set you in a fruitful place. He has also built a tower in the vineyard of your life, and this tower can represent your spirit, the place within you where God comes and abides. When I accepted the Lord Jesus Christ into my life, the Holy Spirit came and took up residence within me. Just as the owner of a vineyard and his family would come into the room at the bottom of the watchtower when it was time to press the grapes, so God is there with me during my trials—my wine press time. Not only does God watch over me to see that I have everything I need to produce good fruit, He is also there to help me when things get tough, when I'm really going through testings and tribulations.

It's the little foxes . . . that can get on our nerves, wear us down, steal our joy and spoil the fruit in our lives.

You see, God looks to my life to produce good fruit, the fruit of the Spirit: love, joy, peace, patience, kindness, goodness, faithfulness, gentleness and self-control (see Gal. 5:22). And that is the fruit of the vine. Jesus said, "I am the vine" (John 15:5). God planted every Christian with the choicest vine, Jesus Christ, that the life of Jesus might manifest those beautiful spiritual fruits that God is looking for in our lives.

Enemies of the Vineyard

The problem, of course, is that vineyards have enemies. That's why, in Isaiah's day, they built the tower with a lookout chamber in the top of it. The watchtower was built by the family who owned the vineyard for very obvious reasons. From that lookout chamber they could see for miles around, watching for any who might try to steal some of the harvest. The Holy Spirit is the one who watches in the towers of our lives, the towers of our spirits. He watches for our enemy, the devil, who seeks to destroy us and the work of God within us. First Peter 5:8 tells us "Your enemy the devil prowls around like a roaring lion looking for someone to devour." The devil delights in devouring and destroying fruit, the fruit of our lives that causes celebration in the heart of God and in the hearts of other people.

Sometimes, when the really *big bears* of life come along—you know, the death of a loved one, divorce, a child who is in trouble or on drugs—God seems to lend us extra courage to cope, and somehow we get through. But it's the *little foxes* of life, those sometimes trivial, nitpicky sources of irritation, the normal everyday problems of living, that can get on our nerves, wear us down, steal our joy and spoil the fruit in our lives. But the whole point of the vineyard is that celebration should be the end result of it, that the wine should be produced—sweet wine, not sour grapes.

Three Ways to Press Grapes

You know, there were three ways to press grapes in Isaiah's day. The first way was that everybody got in and stomped around until the wine ran out. In other words, they trampled the grapes. Have you ever been trampled? I'm a pastor's wife. I've been trampled. People have trampled all over me. Does that mean you should allow people to trample you? No, that's not what I'm saying. But the important thing is, what do you do when people trample you and you can't stop them? The next time you find people trampling on you, why don't you try saying to yourself, Oh, it's wine press time! Then allow God to produce the fruit of patience in your life.

Another way the grapes were pressed in Isaiah's day was to put them in a big stone vat with a huge rock that just pounded them over and over and over again, with no let-up, no break, no variation or change of pace. You know how that is, don't you—that sort of living that we all have to do sometimes: boring, repetitious, with seemingly nothing happening? When you next find yourself in a boring situation where everything seems to be going on and on in unending monotony, remember, it's wine press time. Let God do His work.

The third way that wine can be produced is when the grapes are in such a tight, close bunch that they simply squeeze together and the wine gushes out. Think of yourself as a grape hanging on a bunch. All of us belong to a church, or we should. Have you ever found yourself in a bunch of Christians, squeezed in next to the very grape you can't abide? Well, instead of moaning and groaning about it, why don't you just remind yourself that it's wine press time? God will use that time to produce fruit in your life if you'll just let Him.

It's not how you begin your Christian life that's important, it's how you end it that really matters. We have an ongoing responsibility to keep in touch with the God of life and fruitfulness, and to welcome His wine press times in our lives. If we can do that, then the vineyards of our lives will bring great harvests to the Lord of the vineyard.

SOMETHING TO THINK ABOUT

1. How does your life line up with Hannah's? How can you stop wrestling and pleading and bargaining with God, trying to get what you so desperately desire, and come instead to that place of letting go, of yielding and declaring, Not my will, Lord, but yours?

2. What times in your life can you remember as God's wine press times? How can you, in the future, accept those times and allow Him to produce in you the fruits of the Spirit? How can you be sure that, when God looks out over the vineyard of your life, He will see the makings of sweet wine, rather than sour grapes?

CHAPTER 9

MOUNT OF OLIVES

OBEDIENCE TO THE GREAT COMMISSION

Some time ago, a lady came up to me and said, "Pastor Briscoe, you exasperate me! You are so arrogant."

"I'm sorry to hear that," I replied. "Why do you feel that way?"

"Because you think you have the right to go all over the world and persuade people to become Christians," she answered. "You seem to think that you're so right and everyone else is so wrong, and you've got to impose your views on them."

"Well," I said, "if it's a case of my thinking I'm right and everyone else is wrong, of my imposing my views on them, then I have to agree with you. I am arrogant and I would thoroughly understand that you'd be exasperated with me. However, let me suggest something else to you. Rather than being arrogant, I'm just being obedient."

The Mount of Olives as seen from the Temple area. The Garden of Gethsemane is at the bottom of the Kidron Valley by the church with a mosaic decoration. (Photo © Gilbert Beers)

"To what?" she asked.

"To the Lord Jesus," I answered.

WHAT IS EXPECTED?

The Lord Jesus, if indeed He is Lord, expects His people to obey Him. In Luke 6:46, Jesus asks, "Why do you call me, 'Lord, Lord,' and do not do what I say?" Just what was it that He said? What is it He expects those who call Him Lord to do?

Forty days after His resurrection, Jesus stood on what is often called the Mount of Ascension. It is believed that the site of the Ascension was the Mount of Olives, "a Sabbath day's walk from the city [Jerusalem]" (Acts 1:12). The Mount of Olives lies just east of the Old City of Jerusalem, separated from it by the Kidron Valley.[1] As He stood there on the mountain, Jesus spoke these absolutely profound, challenging words to His disciples: "You will receive power when the Holy Spirit comes on you; and you will be my witnesses in Jerusalem, and in all Judea and Samaria and to the ends of the earth" (Acts 1:8). As soon as He said that, He ascended into heaven and a cloud received Him out of the sight of His disciples.

As the disciples stood there, rooted to the ground and gazing intently toward the sky, two angels spoke to them:

> *"Men of Galilee,"* they said, *"why do you stand here looking into the sky? This same Jesus, who has been taken from you into heaven, will come back in the same way you have seen him go into heaven"* (v. 11).

I've always thought that was one of the most unfair questions ever asked. Fancy asking those men why they

If there is going to be a valid witness, there is also going to be some cost involved.

were standing there, gazing up into heaven! It's pretty obvious, wouldn't you think? If we had been there, I imagine we would have stood there, gazing into heaven right along with the disciples. After all, He was there speaking to them one minute, and the next minute, He was gone! Can't you just hear them asking each other, "Where did He go?" "Did you see Him go?" "Where is He?" "What happened?" Of course, the significance of the angels' statement was to let the disciples know that our Lord Jesus had terminated His earthly ministry, and to reassure them of His promise to return in exactly the same way they had just seen Him go.

A Time to Witness

Now, the time between the conclusion of His earthly ministry and the still forthcoming promise of His return has stretched out over 1,900 years. These have not been years of passive waiting for His return, nor have they been years during which people have forgotten all about Him. They have been years during which Christ has given us the marvelous privilege of fulfilling His last words before He left the earth to ascend back into heaven, what we commonly call the Great Commission: to be His witnesses in Jerusalem, Judea, Samaria, and to the ends of the earth.

It is an awesome and precious thing to be able to be a witness for Jesus. The Greek word for witness is *martus,* from which we also get the word "martyr." Many of the early Christians became martyrs because of their witnessing. That doesn't necessarily mean that if you're going to be a witness today you will automatically become a martyr, but I think it is important to remember that, if there is going to be a valid witness, there is also going to be some cost involved.

*W*e receive the Holy Spirit
in order that we might
articulate and demonstrate that
Jesus Christ is Lord.

Two Ways to Witness

There are two ways of witnessing for Christ. One way is with your lips, articulating your experience of Him as it relates to the truth that He has revealed. Some people are very good articulators. They are open and free, they can think quickly as they speak, they have a good command of words, they have outgoing personalities, they can grab hold of people and get their attention, and they can even make people listen who don't want to listen. But if you're not one of those people, if you're not a good articulator, that does not mean you cannot be a witness for Christ.

When we witness with our lips, we articulate the truth, but in addition to that, we must witness with our lives. Leading a quiet, godly, consistent life is every bit as important in witnessing as being a good articulator. Never underestimate the importance of the witness of your life. You see, to witness for Christ is to live a life-style that exhibits the reality of Christ in the daily things that you do, in the person you are. In fact, we don't have the option of choosing one or the other type of witnessing. Those of us who are good at articulating but who don't live a consistent, winsome, quality-filled life will only end up irritating people in the end. And those of us who live that Christlike life-style, but never explain that Christ is the reason we are able to live that way, will begin to take the glory for ourselves.

In other words, if someone says to me, What a nice person you are! How sweet of you! How generous! if I don't give God the glory with my lips, I am silently taking it for myself. We don't receive the Holy Spirit in order that we might be witnesses to the fact that we are kind and generous and nice. We receive the Holy Spirit in order that we might articulate and demonstrate that Jesus Christ is

Lord, and that it is He who deserves and desires and demands our allegiance, and it is He who is the dynamic of the life that we are living. That was the Great Commission given by the Lord Jesus to His disciples at the conclusion of His earthly ministry.

Where to Witness

I want you to notice also where He told these disciples to go. He told them to start in Jerusalem. That was a very challenging thing to tell those particular disciples, because it was only a few weeks earlier that those same men in that very city, without exception, forsook Him and fled. For them, Jerusalem was the place of their biggest failure. And that's exactly where our Lord sent them first.

Then Jesus talked about Judea. If you've ever been to Judea, you know that it is a blistering wilderness in the summertime. And, at times during the winter, it is so cold you can feel it in your bones. It is not a very pleasant place. But the Lord said, First, I want you to be witnesses for me in the place of your biggest failure, and then I'll send you on to a really tough place.

After that, He told them to go to Samaria. Now, the Jews did not have any dealings with the Samaritans, nor did the Samaritans have anything to do with the Jews. They detested each other. But, you see, the Lord Jesus was challenging His disciples not only to start at the place of their biggest failure and then to go on to a very difficult, unpleasant place, He also wanted them to go where they weren't wanted, where they most assuredly would not be welcomed.

On top of all that, He told them to go out into all the corners of the earth, to all people everywhere, witnessing for Him. There is not one spot on this globe where Jesus Christ is not relevant, and there is not one spot on this globe where He is not needed. The tragedy of the Church is that, at the present time, there are more people in this world than ever before who have not yet been reached with the gospel.

Obedient Witnesses

With that in mind, and remembering that our Lord Jesus commanded us to go into all the world with our witness of Him, then we must recognize something of the most profound importance: the Church of Jesus Christ must produce disciples who will not only go to the places of their failures and witness for Christ, who will tackle the tough places and will go to people who sometimes will not welcome them, but they must also be prepared to uproot and go to every corner of the world to reach the unreached and to teach the untaught. That is our privilege. That is the command given us by our Lord.

We are not being arrogant when we go around trying to persuade people to become Christians; we are being disobedient if we do not! For our Lord Jesus made it quite clear, immediately prior to His ascension, what He expected of His disciples. He expected them to be people who would be witnesses for Him in Jerusalem, Judea, Samaria, and all the corners of the earth.

Faithful Forever

When you think of the privilege it is to be a faithful and bold witness for Christ, have you ever thought of how shameful it is to deny Him? If we are not willing to speak out for our Lord, are we any different from Peter, who, after swearing his undying love and allegiance to Jesus, denied Him? How do you suppose Peter felt after he had denied Him and then, as it tells us in Luke 22:61, "The Lord turned and looked straight at Peter. Then Peter remembered . . . . " What do you suppose Peter remembered? He remembered that he had promised to be faithful to Jesus forever; he also remembered Jesus' words that he (Peter) would deny Him. That look from Jesus broke Peter's heart and "he went outside and wept bitterly" (v. 62).

Jill has written a poem, which I believe captures the heart cry of every disciple who is a witness for Christ, as well as the pain our Lord endured, and the love He so freely gave.

Plaited Crown

by Jill Briscoe

Scourged my King, a plaited crown?
Runs the blood of Godhead down?
Wet the cheeks, the beard pulled out,
ripped the skin and rude the shout.

Hail my King—I'd kiss Thee better
Write authority a letter,
take a picture,
tell the press . . .
All You came to do was bless!
Scourged my King, a plaited crown?
Runs the blood of Godhead down?

Scourged my King— In soldiers' den
Exposed to beasts,
who dressed like men—
Smelt the blood of prey soon caught
Set my Jesus all at naught
Scourged my King, and fool of made
God in Heaven—what price You paid!!

—And all because of my ill health
All my sin and all the wealth

of stupid, dirty, darksome horrors—
past demeanors—black tomorrows.

Scourged my King, a plaited crown?
Runs the blood of Godhead down?

Scourged my King, a plaited crown?
Here I kneel a trembling down—
beat my fists in silent fury
While my world ignores Your story!!

Scourged my King, a plaited crown?

Runs the blood of Godhead down!!!![2]

SOMETHING TO THINK ABOUT

1. Where are you in your journey to fulfill the Great Commission? How can you move on from the point of standing on the Mount of Ascension, gazing up into the heavens and waiting for Him to return, to the point of obedience to Christ's command, making your way into Jerusalem, Judea, Samaria, and every corner of the earth? Even if you cannot physically go anywhere but in your own neighborhood or city, how can you live a life-style there that will be a witness for Christ? And when others notice and comment on that life-style, what can you do or say that will give the glory to God?

2. When was the last time you promised to be faithful to Jesus and then failed? How did you feel when Jesus looked at you, unspeaking, and you realized your failure? Was your heart broken? Did you weep? Remember that, although Peter denied His Lord, although he

failed, he later became a powerful, dynamic witness for Him, to the point of martyrdom. What would it take for you to develop that kind of attitude, that level of commitment?

SECTION FOUR

CHARACTERISTICS OF A DISCIPLE

CHAPTER 10

MOUNT OF THE BEATITUDES

LEARNING ABOUT BLESSEDNESS

High above the beautiful and usually placid, tranquil Sea of Galilee (also known as Lake Tiberias, through which the Jordan River flows), rises the mountain commonly known as the Mount of the Beatitudes. It was here, in this remote, secluded part of the world, that the most dynamic revolution of all time began.

TEACHING THE DISCIPLES ABOUT BLESSEDNESS

One day, as the Lord Jesus looked out on the crowds who were following Him, He saw them as sheep without a shepherd, and He responded by doing a remarkable thing. He called a handful of the most unlikely people imaginable—Simon Peter and his brother Andrew; James

A view of the Sea of Galilee as seen from the probable location of the Sermon on the Mount. (Photo © Stacey Martin)

and John, the sons of Zebedee (also known as the Sons of Thunder)—and promised these poor, uneducated fishermen that He would make them fishers of men (see Matt. 4:19).

You see, His principle of reaching the masses was the old principle of first reaching and training and equipping a dedicated nucleus. Once He had His little group together, with His eyes still on the multitudes and His heart still full of compassion for them, He made His way up the mountainside, bringing His new disciples with Him. There He began to teach them (see Matt. 5:1,2). What He taught them is something that every single disciple of Jesus Christ needs to know and to bear in mind at all times.

The Message of Blessedness

You see, what He taught His disciples was not just for them, it was for all the multitudes who had so moved the heart of the Lord Jesus as He looked out upon them. It is for all the multitudes of people who have walked the face of the earth throughout all the ages, as well as for those of us who are here now, and those yet to come. The message He gave, which we refer to as the Sermon on the Mount, repeats the same word over and over again: blessed. The word *beatitude* in Latin means *blessed are,* and that was the heart of the message the Lord Jesus gave His disciples that day.

The Meaning of Blessedness

Christians use that word a lot, have you ever noticed that? At the end of a Sunday morning service, people often come up to me and say, "Thank you, Pastor, I was really blessed by your sermon." One Sunday, I decided to find out what they meant by that, so when one little lady came up to me and said, "Oh, thank you! I was so blessed by your sermon this morning," I asked her, "What does that mean?"

She looked at me dumbfounded, and replied, "To be perfectly honest, I really don't know." I'm afraid that's how it often is with some of our biblical, ecclesiastical terminology. We use the terms so easily and liberally, without ever stopping to think about their meaning.

Let me tell you about the word "blessed." The Greek word for blessed is *makarios,* which was the word the ancient Greeks used to describe the conditions of the gods as they envisaged them. They thought the gods had it made. They thought that if you could envisage the perfect life, the complete life, the whole life, the full life, it would be makarios, blessed. And that is the word we have here in the Sermon on the Mount.

The Right Kind of Blessedness

Our Lord Jesus had gathered His disciples around Him on the mountainside, overlooking the Sea of Galilee, preparing to teach them what they needed to know in order that they might then go to the masses of people who were wandering like sheep without a shepherd and teach them about the full life, the life of blessedness. The interesting thing about all of this is that when you look at the kind of blessedness that Jesus speaks about on the Sermon on the Mount, it seems to be just the opposite of what you would usually think of as being a blessed life.

For instance, He says, "Blessed are the poor in spirit" (Matt. 5:3, *KJV*). Now, who wants to be poor? Then He says, "Blessed are they that mourn" (v. 4, *KJV*). Who wants to mourn? "Blessed are the meek" (v. 5, *KJV*). Did you ever wake up in the morning and think, Today I want to be meek? "Blessed are they which do hunger and thirst" (v. 6, *KJV*). Do you enjoy being hungry and

He (Jesus) still wants to get across to His disciples that kind of blessedness that is so different from what the world has to offer.

thirsty? When you look at the way our Lord Jesus tackled the teaching of blessedness, it is very easy to see why what He had to say was utterly revolutionary.

One of the sad things about the contemporary church is that it has lost its sense of revolution. It has lost its sense of being a dynamic alternative to the world's society. The masses still wander like sheep without a shepherd. Our Lord still has a heart full of compassion for them. He still wants to get across to His disciples that kind of blessedness that is so different from what the world has to offer, and He still wants to get across to them the principles on which this blessedness works.

The Way to Blessedness

"Blessed are the poor in spirit," He said, "for theirs is the kingdom of heaven. Blessed are they that mourn: for they shall be comforted. Blessed are the meek: for they shall inherit the earth. Blessed are they which do hunger and thirst after righteousness: for they shall be filled" (vv. 3-6, *KJV*). What He was really talking about here was the heart attitude of His disciples. There are some people who are not poor in spirit, they are self-sufficient. They are not poor in spirit, they are self-centered. They are not poor in spirit, they have decided on their own what they are going to do with their lives, and they are bent on getting their own way. They really believe that they have what it takes. In fact, they have been encouraged to believe just that. They live in a society that tells them, If you're going to get anywhere in this world, you've got to get out there and make things happen.

Jesus said that is not the way to blessedness; it is the way to arrogance, the way to self-conceit, but it is not the way to blessedness. You see, what we have to do is be realistic before God about our own spiritual condition. If we are realistic before God concerning our own spiritual condition, we will say to God, I may be doing great by society's standards, but by your standards, I have to admit that I am spiritually impoverished; and, God, that concerns me.

When I realize that I am spiritually impoverished, then I can simply shrug my shoulders and say, Well, that's just how it is. After all, I'm only human! What did you expect? Or, I can begin to mourn about my impoverished state. I can come before the Lord and say, Lord, it deeply disturbs and distresses me that I am so spiritually impoverished. It deeply concerns me that I have fallen so far short of your standards. I come before you now and I mourn my spiritual impoverishment.

The Attitude of Blessedness

At that point, of course, I will be led into another kind of attitude; for, if I understand how spiritually impoverished I am, if I am prepared to mourn my spiritual impoverishment, then I can simply come to the Lord and say, Lord, I want to be meek about this. Now, a lot of people think that meek means weak. It doesn't. Meek means to be yielded, to be submissive. In other words, if I know I am spiritually impoverished, if I mourn my spiritual impoverishment and if I yield myself to the Lord to do something about it, I am beginning to develop the right kind of attitude, that revolutionary attitude that the Lord Jesus wanted to instill in His disciples. This will then lead me to a desire for something different—a desire for righteousness, a righteousness that leads to a desire to get right with God, and to live rightly before Him continually.

Now, everyone hungers and everyone thirsts after something. But what an exciting thing it is to find those true disciples who, being poor in spirit, mourn about their

A *disciple who has learned . . .*
blessed living is indeed
ready to go out and teach the
masses.

spiritual poverty, yield themselves to the Lord, and have an insatiable desire to be right with God and to continually live rightly before God. A disciple who has learned that kind of blessed living is indeed ready to go out and teach the masses.

SOMETHING TO THINK ABOUT

1. What do you think of as a blessed life? Does your definition line up with the standards of the world and its society, or with God's standards? How will your definition of a blessed life lead to a meek spirit and a heart yielded to God?
2. What has happened in your life that has caused you to come before God and admit your spiritual impoverishment? If you have never recognized and mourned your spiritual poverty, what can you do now to seek a change of attitude, an attitude that will lead you to a desire to get right with God and to live rightly before Him continually?

CHAPTER 11

MOUNT OF THE BEATITUDES

LEARNING ABOUT THE KINGDOM

Learning how to live a life of true blessedness wasn't all that Jesus taught the disciples on the Mount of the Beatitudes. It was only the beginning. He wanted them to know that, once they had taken those revolutionary steps toward blessedness, a promise would follow—the promise that they would inherit the Kingdom. He also promised them that they would be comforted, that they would inherit the earth and that they would be filled.

Teaching the Disciples About Kingdom Living

Jesus sat on the Mount of the Beatitudes, His heart moved with compassion for the multitudes wandering like sheep without a shepherd, and He taught His disciples the principles of Kingdom living. We, as disciples today, need to learn those principles if we are ever going to change the multitudes.

The Difference of Kingdom Living

It is important to remember that those disciples who sat at the feet of Jesus, listening to the Sermon on the Mount, were not irreligious men. On the contrary, they were deeply religious people, a product of the Jewish society all around them. The problem with the Jewish society at that particular time, however, was that it was locked into ritual. It was formalistic in its outlook. It was obsessed with externals. *Read Matt 6: 1-18*

In His teaching, the Lord Jesus hit hard at three very important aspects of the Jewish spiritual experience. The Jews were familiar with the principle of fasting. They were familiar with the principle of praying. And they were familiar with the principle of giving alms. The trouble with these three things was that the extreme people in Judaism at that time prayed ostentatiously. They wanted everyone to know how deeply pious they were and that they were spending time in prayer. Jesus told them that they shouldn't pray that way; they shouldn't stand on the street corners, blowing their trumpets and calling, "Look at me, I'm praying!" (see Matt. 6:5-7).

He also told them that when they were fasting, they shouldn't cover themselves with sackcloth and ashes, making themselves appear morose and deprived, and going around with long faces so everyone would say, "Ah, there is someone who is fasting!" (see vv. 16-18). And when they have alms, He told them to be very, very careful not to make their giving known, because if they were giving to receive the praises of men, then that would be their only reward (see vv. 1-4).

The probable site of the Sermon on the Mount as seen from the west. (Photo © Gilbert Beers)

If we identify our existing anxieties, we have identified our priorities.

The Realities of Kingdom Living

In other words, our Lord Jesus was trying to get across to His disciples that it was possible to be very religious on the outside, yet still have a spiritual vacuum on the inside. What He was looking for was spiritual reality—not an external demonstration of fasting, but a willingness to deny oneself the satisfaction of legitimate pleasures for the sake of the kingdom. That is true fasting. Not giving to impress others, but giving out of a heart of concern and compassion, sharing that which God has given in order that others might be blessed—that is true giving of alms. Not praying loudly to be noticed and appear spiritual, but praying out of a desire to commune with the Father—that is true prayer.

The Priorities of Kingdom Living

Our priorities tell us a lot about ourselves. It is very obvious, when our Lord gathered His little nucleus of disciples around Him on the hillside with the view of changing them in order to send them out to change the multitudes, that those disciples had to have different priorities from the rest of society.

Now, we all have priorities. We can identify our existing priorities very easily. Jesus showed us how when he talked about anxieties (see Matt. 6:19-34). Anxieties identify priorities. If we are anxious about something, it's because it is important to us. It is a priority. What were they anxious about in those days? Well, they were anxious about what they should wear. They were anxious about what they should eat. They were anxious about their money. And they were anxious about how long they were going to live. Nothing has changed very much, has it? You see, if we identify our existing anxieties, we have identified our existing priorities.

Then there are activities. I think it's safe to say that we can usually find time to do what we really want to do. And that is certainly the case when our Lord was speaking to the people as recorded in Matthew, chapter 6. He said that they were busy laying up treasures for themselves on earth (see v. 19). They were busy, busy, busy! Now, when we're that busy doing something, we are busily active in a priority.

And what about ambitions? What about the time we spend on the things we desire—what we long to be, what we long to do—those, too, are priorities. So, at any given moment, we can easily identify our priorities. Once we've identified them, we need to evaluate them.

As far as food is concerned, Jesus said, How about looking at the birds? They seem to be doing all right. The birds of the air seem to be cared for by our heavenly Father (see v. 26). As for what to wear, the lilies of the field are beautifully adorned. The Father seems to take care of their needs, as well (see v. 28). So what about finances? Jesus said, to protect your finances from the moths and the rust and the thieves (He could have added inflation and taxes to that list), store up your treasures in heaven (see v. 20). Why? "For where your treasure is, there your heart will be also" (v. 21).

You see, it is so easy to get wrapped up in our priorities without ever having evaluated them. But, when we take the time to stop and evaluate them, we begin to discover that we have all the important things in the unimportant category, and all the unimportant things in the important category. Everything is backwards!

The Establishment of Kingdom Listing

Now, Jesus told His disciples, Get your priorities straight. They may then have asked, How do we do that? That's

*T*he old self . . . is going to
have to get off the throne . . .
that . . . we (might) establish the
Kingdom of God in our hearts.

when Jesus came out with the marvelous statement, "But seek first his kingdom and his righteousness, and all these things will be given to you as well" (v. 33). In other words, we must make absolutely certain that God, reigning as King in our personal lives, is our first priority. That's going to mean that the old self, that ego, is going to have to get off the throne in order that God, through the risen Christ, might be Lord and Master of our lives. When we do that, we establish the Kingdom of God in our hearts.

But Jesus didn't mean that the Kingdom should be established in our hearts only; He meant that the Kingdom should be demonstrated in our lives, too. When we are members of the Kingdom of God, we will behave like sons and daughters of the King. That should become a priority.

Not only that, but Jesus said that, before the end of the world comes, the gospel of the Kingdom must first be preached as a witness to all nations (see Matt. 24:14). That, too, must be a priority. I want to make certain that the Kingdom is established in my heart. That's a priority. I want to behave like a child of the King. That's a priority. And I want to make absolutely certain that I'm involved in the expansion of the Kingdom before the end comes. That's a priority.

The Commitment of Kingdom Living

Now, our Lord said that when we get these priorities established in our lives, all these other things we worry about—food, clothing, finances, health—will also come to us. He doesn't say these things are unimportant, but He wants us to see that they are of much less importance than the things of the Kingdom.

There are some people who understand this and, because they do, they are prepared to utterly commit themselves to the Lord. And, when they utterly commit themselves to Him, they have also committed to Him their anxieties about what to eat, what to wear, and even where they will obtain sufficient finances. They do this on the understanding that the Lord Himself will take care of all of those things because they have made the Kingdom of God their first priority.

The Changes of Kingdom Living

Can you see what a radical change was taking place in the disciples as they began to understand what the Lord was saying? He was changing them so that they might go out into society in the name of Christ and change it.

The Lord ended His teaching with a simple little story. He told His disciples about two men, one of whom built his house on sand, the other on solid rock. When the storm came, the house on the sand disintegrated, but the house on the rock stood firm. He told them that those who hear His teaching and adhere to it are like people who build their houses on rock. But those who hear His teaching and walk away and ignore it are like those who build their houses on sand—everything will eventually come crashing down around them (see Matt. 7:24-27).

Our Lord Jesus saw the multitudes. His heart ached with compassion for them. So He called His disciples, brought them up on the hillside, sat them down and taught them radical doctrine, doctrine that would require them to be totally committed to Him. Increasingly, they began to understand His words and, as they did, their lives were given over to Him and He wrought a wonderful change in their hearts. This change was particularly evident later on, after they understood the significance of the death and resurrection of Jesus, after the Spirit of God had come into their lives.

Jesus had begun to change them from within and, as

they moved out from the mountainside by the Sea of Galilee into the far corners of the world, the revolution began. It hasn't ended yet. One of the glorious privileges of those of us who call ourselves disciples of Christ is, through the power of the Holy Spirit within, putting the principles of the Sermon on the Mount into practice in our lives so that we, being changed, might be agents of change in our contemporary society.

SOMETHING TO THINK ABOUT

1. When did you last take the time to identify your priorities? Stop now and make a list of those things that cause you anxiety, those things you do because you enjoy doing them, and those things you spend time seeking to obtain. What does your list tell you about your priorities?

2. How strong is your commitment to the Kingdom of God? What can you do to insure that your desire to see the Kingdom established in your life is strong enough so that you can put aside your anxieties and trust God to take care of them as you go about His business?

As you leave, think about some of our personal ambitions, activities, or anxieties that may be crowding God's Kingdom for first place in our life.

CHAPTER 12

JERUSALEM

APPROPRIATING HIS POWER

The quiet, unchanging beauty of present-day Galilee is a reminder of the days our Lord spent there, patiently and carefully teaching His disciples. But Jesus had to leave Galilee, the place of tranquil teaching, and move on to Jerusalem, the place for rugged, determined action.

THE REASON FOR HIS COMING

Luke 9:51 tells us, "As the time approached for him to be taken up to heaven, Jesus resolutely set out for Jerusalem." I particularly like the way the King James Version puts it: "He stedfastly set his face to go to Jerusalem." Have you ever steadfastly set your face to go somewhere or to do something? You know the look. Your jaw is set,

your mind is made up, and your eyes have that determined look. Whatever else may come your way, you will not be deterred from accomplishing your goal.

That was the look on Jesus' face as He set out for Jerusalem, knowing full well what lay ahead. It was the reason for His coming, the purpose of His incarnation. And so, steadfastly setting His face for Jerusalem, He began His journey.

Because the Jews and Samaritans were mutually antagonistic, it was customary for Galileans to circumvent Samaria, even though it was the quickest and most direct route to Jerusalem. Instead, they traveled down the ancient Jordan Valley. As our Lord walked this historic route, no doubt He thought of the dramatic crossing of the same river by the ancient people of Israel. Passing through Jericho, He began the long hot climb through the barren wilderness, which eventually brought Him to Jerusalem, the place of tragedy and the scene of triumph.

It's ironic, isn't it, that, in modern-day Jerusalem, the site of Calvary—Golgotha, the place of the skull—is situated by the bus station. Yet, on second thought, it may be an appropriate reminder that, when Christ died, the masses went on with their daily work and play, oblivious to the significance of the event that was taking place.

Another spot in Jerusalem I would like to mention is the Garden Tomb. My mother-in-law used to say, "You're closer to God's heart in a garden than anywhere else on earth." I think she may well have been right about gardens in general, but certainly this one in particular. The Garden Tomb is situated in a lovely, quiet little garden, located in

The Garden Tomb in Jerusalem, which may have been the site of Jesus' burial. (Photo by Frances Blankenbaker)

The Resurrection . . . demonstrated the sheer power of God that is available to all Christians.

the midst of hustling, bustling, modern Jerusalem. No one knows exactly where Jesus was crucified and no one knows exactly where His body was laid; therefore, no one knows exactly the scene where He rose again from the dead. However, all things considered, the Garden Tomb may well be that very place.

SUBSTANTIATING HIS CLAIMS

Now, Jesus, during His earthly ministry, made all sorts of dramatic statements concerning Himself. These remarkable claims were either utterly stupid, or they were totally stupendous. For instance, He said, "I am the way and the truth and the life. No one comes to the Father except through me" (John 14:6). On another occasion, He said, "I and the Father are one" (John 10:30). When He was asked if He was truly the Son of God, He answered, "Yes, it is as you say" (Matt. 26:64). Another time, He said, "Before Abraham was born, I am!" (John 8:58).

Keeping in mind these claims, think about the Resurrection for a moment. The fact that Jesus rose again from the dead gives credibility to His remarkable claims; it is also the most dramatic demonstration of God's power imaginable. Paul, writing to the Ephesian Christians, prayed that they might really grasp the power of God in their lives, understand it and experience it (see Eph. 1:17-19). When he wanted to illustrate that power, he said, "That power is like the working of his mighty strength, which he exerted in Christ when he raised him from the dead and seated him at his right hand in the heavenly realms" (vv. 19,20). So, as far as Paul was concerned, the Resurrection not only substantiated the claims of our Lord Jesus, it also demonstrated the sheer power of God that is available to all Christians.

HOPE FOR THE HOPELESS

Moreover, when we think in terms of the resurrection of Jesus, we're reminded of the glorious fact that there is hope after the tomb. So many people spend their lives in hopelessness. They hope that everything will work out all right, but it doesn't. They get sick, then hope the doctors can cure them; they can't. So they hope someone else will come up with a cure in time, but they don't. They hope they won't die, but they recognize that they are going to die. And they go on hoping where there's no hope.

But the glorious message of the Resurrection is that, once you're dead, you're not finished! Jesus, having died, came back from the dead and gave us the assurance that there is life after death. Not only that, He promises that He will take us to be with Him (see John 14:3). The Scriptures also tell us that the risen Christ, in the person of the Holy Spirit, will come to live within our hearts and will give us the awesome power of God to enable us to fulfill the demands of God upon us (see Acts 1:8).

Some people think that the demands of God are unreasonable, and they're right, if Christ is not risen. But, if Christ is risen and indwelling us by His Spirit, then He is making demands upon us that are equated to the power of God made available to us. That's why Paul insisted, wherever he went, that Jesus Christ is risen from the dead. That was his message over and over again. He is risen from the dead and, therefore, substantiates His claims. He is risen from the dead and, therefore, illustrates God's power. He is risen from the dead and, therefore, gives hope of life after the grave. He is risen from the dead and, therefore, in the person of the Holy Spirit, gives us the dynamic to meet the demands of God upon us. No wonder Paul wouldn't allow anyone to suggest that there was no such thing as the Resurrection! No wonder that, wherever he went, he proclaimed the risen Christ!

PROOF OF HIS POWER

But why did Paul believe this? Why do Christians believe in the Resurrection? Well, let me take you back about 1,900 years to Jerusalem, possibly to the Garden Tomb or, at least, somewhere very near that spot. Now, let me remind you of three important pieces of information that were available to anyone who lived in Jerusalem at that time. First, Jesus had died; second, His body was taken from the cross by Joseph of Arimathea and Nicodemus, and laid in a tomb belonging to Joseph of Arimathea's family. Jesus was laid in the tomb, but when visitors came to the garden, the body was not in the tomb. What happened to the missing body?

The third piece of information was the existence of persistent rumors that Jesus had appeared to various people at different times, in numerous places, under widely divergent circumstances.

In addition to these three pieces of information, there is the evidence that, after the Resurrection, our Lord's disciples were dramatically transformed; they were wonderfully changed.

His Body Was Missing

Now, these pieces of information need to be carefully evaluated and explained. Many had witnessed His death. But where was the body? Some people say the disciples stole it. Why would the disciples steal His body, then preach that Christ had died and risen from the dead, even when that very preaching meant martyrdom? If the story

The Holy Spirit . . . gives us the dynamic to meet the demands of God upon us.

of His resurrection were not true, they would have backed down under the threat of death.

Others say the Jewish authorities took the body because they didn't want His grave to become a shrine. But we must remember that the Jewish people wanted to stamp out this new sect who called themselves followers of the Way. What better way to do that than to stop all the nonsensical talk of a Resurrection? All they had to do was present the body. Why didn't they present the body? Because they simply did not have it.

He Really Died

No, we cannot say that the disciples stole the body, and we cannot say that the Jews stole the body. So then, some people would have us believe that He wasn't really dead. After the scourging and the whipping, after the cruelty of the crucifixion, after He had been proclaimed dead by the expert executioners, after He had actually had His heart pierced by a spear, was laid in a tomb, wrapped in grave clothes, left in the tomb for three days and three nights without water, food or fresh air, they want us to believe that he suddenly revived, unwrapped Himself from the grave clothes, rolled away the stone that the women knew they couldn't move themselves, and then disappeared without the guards even noticing it.

He Was Not a Hypocrite

And then, of course, we would have to believe that Jesus allowed the phony story of His resurrection to be propagated around the world, knowing full well it wasn't true. That would make Him the biggest hypocrite this world has ever seen!

No, that isn't what happened to the body. What happened to the body was that Jesus did exactly what He said

He would do: He rose from the dead (see Matt. 16:21). How else do we account for the reports of His appearances after His death?

He Appeared to Many

Well, some people say they were not actual appearances, merely hallucinations. Others call it wish fulfillment, or maybe a psychic phenomenon. But I believe we have to look at the information available to us and recognize that all those explanations are highly unlikely for the simple reason that there were many reported appearances under many different circumstances. Sometimes He appeared to just one person, sometimes to two, sometimes to eleven or twelve. On at least one occasion, He appeared to an excess of 500 people at the same time (see 1 Cor. 15:5,6). Could all those people in all those different circumstances and situations have been hallucinating?

Transformed Disciples

Now, I'm not asking anyone to believe that Jesus rose again from the dead just because of the reported sightings. But, when you combine the information concerning the missing body and the information concerning the appearances, then add to that the information concerning the transformed disciples—like Peter, who couldn't witness to a little girl just before our Lord's death; then, seven weeks later, preached so effectively that vast crowds were converted—you come up with some pretty solid grounds for believing that what Jesus said he would do, He actually did. Jesus rose from the dead. And when He did, that same Resurrection power became available to all who would call on His Name.

Confronted by the Risen Christ

The apostle Paul said, Christ lives in me. He is my life (see

Phil. 1:21). "Christ has indeed been raised from the dead," Paul declared in 1 Corinthians 15:20. All of that really crystallized for Paul (formerly Saul of Tarsus) that day when he left Jerusalem through the Damascus Gate, heading out to Damascus to persecute the followers of the Way. It was there that he was confronted by the risen Christ. From there he went forward to proclaim the resurrection of Jesus Christ for the rest of his days.

The Garden Tomb—is that the spot where Jesus was buried? Is it the same garden where the women came to anoint the body of Jesus? The same garden where Mary saw Jesus, mistaking Him for the gardener? We don't know for sure, but we do know that Mary stood weeping in the garden, thinking that someone had taken away the body of her Lord (see John 20:11-13). What incredible, indescribable joy must have filled her heart when she realized that Jesus was no longer in the tomb, that it was not the gardener standing before her—it was her risen, living Lord!

The Gardener

by Jill Briscoe

She knew He was dead.
She had watched Him die,
hanging between
the earth and sky.
She knew He was dead.
She had heard Him scream
as the guilt of our sin
had come in between
Himself and His God,
as the punishment rod

fell to chastise
His choicest prize.
She knew He was dead,
so pardon her
for thinking Him only
the gardener.
He called her name.
He was just the same,
save the light in His eyes
and His spear-pierced frame.
The love and the light
in His eyes was too much,
and the sense and the power
of His risen life-touch.
Dear Lord, Dear Lord,
please pardon her
for thinking you only
the gardener!
Many folks that I know
have a Jesus of gloom,
alive, yet confined
to their garden tomb.
They worship a memory,
a man of some fame,
but He never called them
by their very own name.
Dear Lord, Dear Lord,
be the pardoner
for thinking you only
a gardener!
Look into His face,
let go of His feet,
stop trying to wrap Him
in that winding sheet!

He isn't a fable,
a ghost or a fake.
He's Jesus, your Saviour,
and He rose for your sake. [1]

SOMETHING TO THINK ABOUT

1. What does the Resurrection mean to you? How did you feel when you came face to face with the risen power of Christ? When you saw Him, did you mistake Him for the gardener because you were still thinking of Jesus as being in the tomb? Or did you cry out to Him in recognition, rejoicing that you had a risen, living Savior?
2. How can you begin to appropriate that Resurrection power in your own life? How can it help you meet the demands of God upon your life right now?

EPILOGUE

We have arrived at the end of our trip through *The Journey of a Disciple.* But our journey as disciples of Jesus Christ continues each day of our lives as we learn to follow, learn to listen, and learn to trust the Master. The journey is not easy, but Jesus never said it was going to be easy. Let us endeavor to please Him in every way so that He can say, "Well done, good and faithful servant" (Matt. 25:21).[1]

NOTES

Chapter 3
1. Jill Briscoe, "No More Grey" in *Wings* (Nashville, TN: Thomas Nelson Publishers, 1984), © 1984 by Briscoe Ministries. Used by author permission.

Chapter 6
1. *The New Encyclopaedia Britannica*, © 1987 Encyclopaedia Britannica, Inc., Vol. 3, Micropaedia, p. 731.

Chapter 7
1. *The New Encyclopaedia Britannica*, © 1987 Encyclopaedia Britannica, Inc., Vol. 6, Micropaedia, p. 538.

Chapter 8
1. *The New Encyclopaedia Britannica*, © 1987 Encyclopaedia Britannica, Inc., Vol. 10, Micropaedia, p. 739.

Chapter 9
1. *The New Encyclopaedia Britannica*, © 1987 Encyclopaedia Britannica, Inc., Vol. 8, Micropaedia, p. 918.
2. Jill Briscoe, "Plaited Crown" in *Wings* (Nashville, TN: Thomas Nelson Publishers, 1984), © 1984 by Briscoe Ministries. Used by author permission.

Chapter 12
1. Jill Briscoe, "The Gardener" in *A Time for Living* (Nashville, TN: Ideals Publishing Corporation, 1980), © 1980 by Briscoe Ministries. Used by author permission.

Epilogue
1. Study guide for *Journey of a Disciple*, Copyright © 1985 by Journeys of a Disciple, A Limited Partnership. Used by permission.